# A Thousand-Year Rain

## THE HISTORIC FLOOD OF 2013 IN BOULDER AND LARIMER COUNTIES

PRESENTED BY

Published by Pediment Publishing, a division of
The Pediment Group, Inc. www.pediment.com
Printed in Canada

# Foreword

**September is usually one of the driest** and sunniest months along Colorado's Front Range, making it the perfect time for outdoor activities such as golf, running, water sports and hiking. Most residents will tell you the weather in Colorado is one of the reasons they love living here.

The weather in September 2013 started out as one would expect. The first eight days of the month offered sunny skies and warm temperatures, and the residents of the Front Range took full advantage of the beautiful, late-summer weather. No one suspected — not even the meteorologists — that the next seven days would bring rainfall that in some areas would exceed the annual precipitation for the entire year.

Boulder, for example, through October, saw 31.78 inches of precipitation this year, more than half of which fell as rain between Sept. 9 and 16. The city, where the average annual precipitation (rain and melted frozen precipitation) is just 20.68 inches, has already eclipsed its previous annual record of 29.93 inches, set in 1995. Similar record rainfall tallies were recorded along the northern Front Range.

The records are especially noteworthy because, prior to Sept. 9, most of Colorado had been sweltering through long-term drought conditions.

Floods in Colorado are not like flooding disasters in other parts of the country. The mountains are primarily rock with limited vegetation. The volume of rain that fell over Boulder and Larimer counties turned once-gurgling streams and slow-flowing rivers into torrents that tore through towns, ripping houses apart, washing away roads and forever changing the lives of thousands who lived near the waterways. Sadly, nine people across the state died in the flooding. Six of them were our friends and neighbors in Northern Colorado.

The damage was so widespread and unusual that meteorologists referred to the flooding as epic, biblical; they dubbed the storm a once-in-a-1,000-year rain event.

Over the course of the flood, tens of thousands of people were directly affected by flooding, and the number of helicopter rescues was the most since Hurricane Katrina, with more than 1,750 people flown to safety. Official estimates put the number of homes damaged or destroyed at 19,000 statewide, while at least 30 bridges were destroyed and another 20 damaged. In all, property loss from the flooding was estimated at nearly $2 billion.

As with every disaster, the power of the human spirit was proudly on display. That spirit led to hundreds of acts of heroism that came in the form of rescues of all kinds, helping hands of thousands of volunteers and the unending support of law enforcement, fire departments, local governments and hundreds of nonprofit organizations.

The beautiful Colorado weather has returned, but the horrific devastation of the flooding will remain  for many years to come, as thousands repair and rebuild their homes and lives, as communities recover and rebound, roads are repaired and reopened, and waterways move along new streambeds.

This book is an amazing collection – a sampling, really – of photos taken by our incredible photojournalists, documenting a disaster that no one saw coming, a historical record of the once-in-a-1,000-year disaster.

A portion of the profits from the sale of this book will be donated to the Community Foundation of Northern Colorado and the Foothills Flood Relief Fund for Boulder and Broomfield Counties, which will dedicate the money to helping residents all along the Front Range affected by the flood.

Al Manzi
President, Publisher and CEO
Prairie Mountain Media

# Table of Contents

5    A STORM FOR THE AGES

7    BOULDER

33    LONGMONT

59    LYONS

85    MOUNTAIN TOWNS

117    LOVELAND

147    ESTES PARK

158    ACKNOWLEDGMENTS

159    OUR PHOTOJOURNALISTS

160    IN REMEMBRANCE

# A Storm for the Ages

**One expert said the last place he saw a** comparable weather system was India — during monsoon season. Another said it would have been an extraordinary event, even had it occurred in New Orleans.

But this was Colorado. No one who lived through it is likely to ever forget it.

The city of Boulder tied its record high for the date, Sunday, Sept. 8. A high-pressure system fueled the heat and held rainfall to barely more than a trace since the start of the month.

That all changed the morning of Monday, Sept. 9, when a cold front dropped into northeast Colorado, and deep subtropical moisture also moved into the area. By late afternoon, the rain began.

A nearly stationary low-pressure system to the west over the Great Basin started pulling a vigorous plume of monsoonal tropical moisture from the Pacific Ocean off Mexico into our middle and upper atmosphere. As the storm progressed, the counter-clockwise circulation harvested even more moisture at lower altitudes from the Gulf of Mexico. Blocking it all in place was the high-pressure system that drifted eastward, parking over the Midwest.

On Tuesday, Sept. 10, showers and a few heavy storms developed in this extremely moist environment, producing mostly moderate rainfall events up and down the Front Range, with amounts of 0.25 inches to 1.25 inches commonplace, and just over 1 inch falling in Boulder.

Fast-developing upslope energy, fed by cool air streaming into the back side of the high-pressure system to the east, drove the moisture against the Front Range foothills. A stalled front created lift that enhanced pounding rain over the region.

The worst was yet to come.

The 36 hours from the afternoon of Wednesday, Sept. 11, to Friday morning, Sept. 13, saw the storm's greatest fury, as an upper level low in the desert Southwest moved slowly to the north, and deeper subtropical moisture continued shifting to the north and east.

A narrow band of very heavy rain organized late Wednesday north of Denver, marching west toward the foothills, Boulder and Larimer counties squarely in its sights. By 9 p.m., the heaviest showers were dumping up to 2 inches per hour.

Flash flooding increased as midnight neared, and water cascading down every drainage out of the high country compounded the heavy rain pounding every community in the two counties.

The National Weather Service advisory issued at 9:41 a.m. Thursday warned of "biblical" rainfall amounts in many areas, noting, "Things are not looking good."

Rainfall in the heaviest storm cells still neared 1.5 inches per hour. Even when the rain periodically eased, its impact remained powerful on streams already running at historic levels and saturated ground.

The 24-hour period ending at 6 p.m. Thursday saw 9.08 inches of rain drench the Boulder area — the hardest hit during the storm — nearly doubling the previous one-day record, and contributing to a record-shattering 17.18 inches for the month of September.

Before the deluge ended, storm rainfall totals of 13.15 inches would be registered by the NWS at Allenspark, 12.32 inches near Lyons, 9.3 inches at Estes park and 8.19 inches just west of Longmont.

The storm lost its intensity Friday, Sept. 13 — even while flooding continued — and the following day was the first without significant rain since its onset. Sunday, Sept. 15 saw a final burst of heavy showers in the morning, before the storm's wrath was expended.

Weather historians will study the storm for a long time to come, but the NWS reported that, in some locations, rainfall reached a once-in-1,000-year intensity.

The rain of September 2013, in every sense, was a storm for the ages.

— Charlie Brennan, Daily Camera

# CHAPTER ONE

# Boulder

**The alert, posted on the city of Boulder's Facebook page at** 4:50 p.m. Wednesday, Sept. 11, seemed innocuous enough at the time:

"Holy rain Batman! As a result, trails in the Marshall Mesa, Flatirons Vista and Doudy Draw areas south of #Boulder are closed due to muddy conditions."

That message, later recognizable as the first warning to the public from the city of the looming meteorological calamity, concluded with the pledge, "We'll post again once trails are reopened."

It would be weeks before those water-logged trails were reopened to the public.

By the night of Sept. 11, what seemed, at first blush, like nothing more than an unusual stretch of rainy days had transformed into a historic, week-long weather disaster, with floodwaters washing across much of Boulder County, ravaging homes, cutting off entire mountain towns and ultimately claiming four lives countywide.

In Boulder, the city largely was cut off the first two nights, as police and sheriff's deputies closed most major roadways in and out of town after water spilled from swelling creeks and torrential rains pooled everywhere.

Downtown, Boulder Creek raged like a river. "It looked like rapids were running across Central Park," police Chief Mark Beckner later remarked.

And throughout the city, thousands of homeowners and renters struggled against rising waters in basements and yards, then spent days, weeks — for many it will be months still to come — banding together to clean out muck, haul away damaged property and help each other get their lives back in order.

---

**LEFT:** From left, Dan Feldheim, Scott Hoffenberg and John Smart pass sandbags to reinforce the dam on Seventh Street on University Hill in Boulder on Sunday, Sept. 15, when rain fell heavily again and increased fears of more flooding in the community. PAUL AIKEN/DAILY CAMERA

**TOP RIGHT:** Aaron Furman checks on flooded basement apartments in the Aspen Grove Apartments off Kalmia Avenue in north Boulder Thursday morning, Sept. 14. PAUL AIKEN/DAILY CAMERA

**ABOVE:** Eddie Fundingsland rides an inner tube through the tunnel underpass at Colorado and 28th Street just off the University of Colorado campus on Wednesday night, Sept. 11. PAUL AIKEN/DAILY CAMERA

**TOP LEFT:** Dag Larson, right, helps Alek Stefanov gather his belonging from his flooded apartment in the Aspen Grove Apartments off Kalmia Avenue in north Boulder on Thursday morning, Sept. 12. Larson and a friend woke Stefanov from a sound sleep as water poured into his apartment. PAUL AIKEN/DAILY CAMERA

**LEFT:** Stalled vehicles are seen floating on 28th Street near Pearl Street on Thursday, Sept. 12, in Boulder. MATTHEW JONAS/LONGMONT TIMES-CALL

**ABOVE:** A tow crew works to get stranded cars off South Boulder Road after heavy rains overnight caused flooding in Boulder on Thursday, Sept. 12. MARK LEFFINGWELL/DAILY CAMERA

**LEFT:** Jack Templeton stands in knee-deep water while trying to access his storage facility in Boulder after it was flooded by heavy rains on Thursday, Sept. 12. MARK LEFFINGWELL/DAILY CAMERA

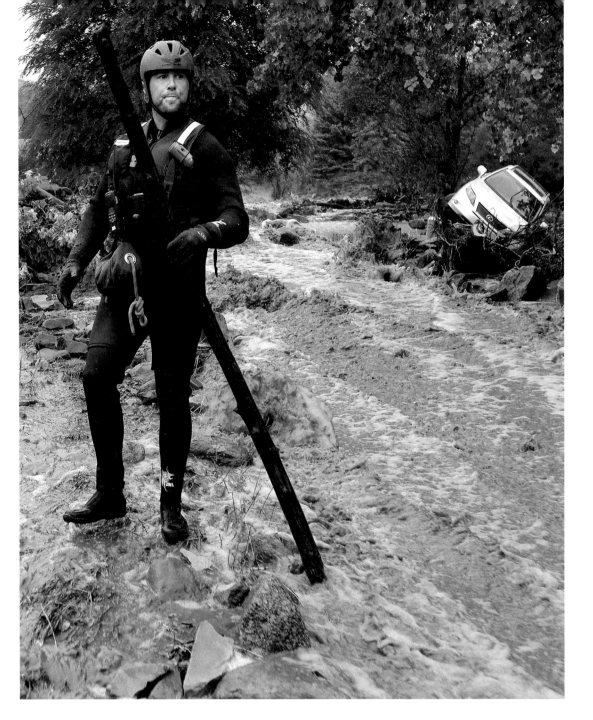

**ABOVE:** North Metro Fire Rescue firefighters wade back to dry ground after assisting in a mandatory evacuation of the Centaur Circle area in Lafayette on Thursday, Sept. 12. DAVID R. JENNINGS/BROOMFIELD ENTERPRISE

**RIGHT:** Brighton Fire Rescue firefighter Clint Mader searches for a possible drowning victim along Linden Avenue in Boulder during the heavy flooding on Thursday, Sept. 12. JEREMY PAPASSO/DAILY CAMERA

**OPPOSITE:** People look at an overturned car near the fast-moving water rushing across the base of Linden Avenue in Boulder during the heavy flooding on Thursday, Sept. 12. JEREMY PAPASSO/DAILY CAMERA

**ABOVE:** Jake Bennett moves a sandbag to help funnel water down Seventh Street at University Boulevard as heavy rains cause severe flooding throughout Boulder on Sept. 12.

MARK LEFFINGWELL/DAILY CAMERA

**TOP:** Trent Fallica, of the city of Boulder Traffic Signal Department, checks an electrical box next to a raging creek during the early flooding in north Boulder on Thursday morning, Sept. 12. PAUL AIKEN/DAILY CAMERA

**ABOVE:** A man photographs flooding in the underpass at Boulder Creek and Broadway. CLIFF GRASSMICK/DAILY CAMERA

# Daily Camera

Levy leaving Colorado Legislature, Local 1B  Syria to offer weapons data, World View 2A

Friday, September 13, 2013 • $1.00 • www.dailycamera.com

# 100-YEAR FLOOD

## President Barack Obama approves federal disaster aid

By Brittany Anas
Camera Staff Writer

President Barack Obama signed an emergency order Thursday night, approving federal disaster aid for Boulder County after torrential rainfall prompted 100-year flooding that has, so far, resulted in two confirmed deaths, at least nine more missing and National Guard rescue efforts.

Continued flooding caused dozens more evacuations throughout the county, power outages and the closure of U.S. 36 on Thursday. Parts of most major roads in Boulder were also closed.

Walls of water coming down canyons triggered mudslides and structure collapses and buildings to be swept away — especially in Jamestown and Fourmile Canyon. The city of Boulder issued an emergency declaration allowing officials to seek support from the state and the Federal Emergency Management Agency.

As of late Thursday night, nine people were reported missing in Boulder, with their family members or friends unable to locate them. More than 400 officers throughout the county were performing search-and-rescue operations, said Gabrielle Boerkircher, a county spokeswoman.

Officials declined to release the missing persons list for fear citizens would try to go on rogue, dangerous search-and-rescue missions.

"We're all pretty much locked in Boulder right now," Boerkircher said. "The main

See **DEPUTIES, 5A**

**Sahand Tabatabi** tries to untangle debris that washed down to his home near Tamarack Avenue and Broadway after heavy rains caused severe flooding in Boulder. For more photos and videos of the flood, go to www.dailycamera.com.

Mark Leffingwell | Daily Camera

**Tow truck workers** attach a cable to a car after a bridge collapse on a business access road at U.S. 287 and Dillon Road in Lafayette caused three vehicles to fall in the creek.

Cliff Grassmick | Daily Camera

**Britt Drake** stands in her flooded basement Thursday in Boulder.

Jeremy Papasso | Daily Camera

## Flooding claims at least two lives in Boulder, Jamestown

By Mitchell Byars
Camera Staff Writer

The massive flooding across Boulder County has claimed the lives of at least two people and left one woman missing, and officials fear more casualties may be discovered as crews begin to make their way into the mountain towns and heavily affected areas.

The first casualty was a man who was killed in a structure collapse in James-

a man killed in the 200 block of Linden Drive in Boulder later that morning after being swept away in his car. A woman who was with that victim is now also missing.

While those are the only two confirmed fatalities, Boulder County Sheriff Joe Pelle said officials are worried that as crews begin cleanup efforts, more casualties could be discovered.

"We're bracing for the worst," Pelle said.

## Dueling weather systems swamp rainfall records

Storm qualifies as 100-year flood event as creek levels rise

By Charlie Brennan
Camera Staff Writer

A complex confluence of

rain that claimed lives, destroyed homes and ruined personal property — and, as it pounded on for days, shattered local records for moisture.

Longstanding rainfall records were swept away in what an official with the United States Geological Survey late Thursday confirmed was for Boulder a 100-year flood

### More flood coverage

• See up-to-the-minute coverage of developments in the flood at www.dailycamera.com
• See in pictures how the rain is affecting Boulder County, Page 6A
• Lyons and east county residents forced to evacuate, Page 7A
• CU, other schools closed today, dealing with damage, Page 2A
• The big Boulder flood could hurt local farms, Page 15A

**To our readers:**

Due to the extreme weather, some deliveries may be delayed or simply impossible.

We apologize for the inconvenience and appreciate your understanding.

So that you do not miss today's edition, we have made our online replica edition available for free at boulderdailycamera.co.newsmemory.com
— Kevin Kaufman, editor

### Weather

High: 74° | Low: 54°

Complete index

**LEFT:** An unidentified man tries to untangle debris that washed down to his home after heavy rains caused severe flooding in Boulder on Thursday, Sept. 12. MARK LEFFINGWELL/DAILY CAMERA

**BOTTOM LEFT:** Kent Shorrock, a Daily Camera staffer, center, and his wife Astrid Paustian get help from Patrick Truman moving straw bales to divert floodwaters away from their home along Violet Avenue in North Boulder on Friday morning, Sept. 13. PAUL AIKEN/DAILY CAMERA

**BOTTOM RIGHT:** Jim Thomas uses patio stones to hold back floodwaters from his home off Lee Hill Drive in Boulder on Friday, Sept. 13. PAUL AIKEN/DAILY CAMERA

**OPPOSITE:** A bridge collapse on a business access road at U.S. 287 and Dillon Road in Lafayette caused three cars to crash into the flooded creek Thursday, Sept. 12. CLIFF GRASSMICK/DAILY CAMERA

**ABOVE:** Kyle Schuler, left, carries his pregnant sister with the help of their father, Kim, after gathering belongings from their flooded home on Upland Avenue in Boulder on Friday, Sept. 13. JEREMY PAPASSO/DAILY CAMERA

**TOP RIGHT:** Dave Naber, left, and Kelly Schultz shovel mud and water out of one of the Farmers Insurance offices on west Arapahoe on Friday, Sept. 13. CLIFF GRASSMICK/DAILY CAMERA

**RIGHT:** Kyle Lamy carries baby seats and a carrier from a friend's home in Pine Brook Hills. Lamy's friend and his wife had to be evacuated from their home, and shortly after their baby was born. Lamy and other friends of the couple went up to check on their home and get baby items on Friday, Sept. 13. PAUL AIKEN/DAILY CAMERA

**OPPOSITE TOP:** Greg Leon looks at an overturned car in Pine Brook Hills on Friday Sept. 13. PAUL AIKEN/DAILY CAMERA

**OPPOSITE BOTTOM LEFT:** Teenagers Wiyanna Nelson and Wesley Quinlan died when they tried to escape from this car after it was overwhelmed by floodwaters in Pine Brook Hills. PAUL AIKEN/DAILY CAMERA

**OPPOSITE BOTTOM RIGHT:** A section of North Cedar Brook Drive in Pine Brook Hills was washed out by the raging floodwaters. PAUL AIKEN/DAILY CAMERA

**TOP LEFT:** A ground crew assists a woman rescued from one the mountain towns from a National Guard helicopter at Boulder Municipal Airport in Boulder on Saturday, Sept. 14. Many small mountain towns were cut off from road access and people could only be brought out by air. MARK LEFFINGWELL/DAILY CAMERA

**TOP RIGHT:** Amia Hensberry, 21 months, gives her mother, Karina, a potato chip from her meal served by CU Athletes to residents of the university's Family Housing in the Club Room at Folsom Stadium. CU had an abundance of food after the Buff's football game Saturday, Sept. 14, was cancelled because of the flooding. DAVID R. JENNINGS/BROOMFIELD ENTERPRISE

**RIGHT:** Bonnie Dannelly, left, hugs her daughter Makayla after she got off the bus at Fireside Elementary in Louisville on Saturday, Sept. 14. Makayla was one of the more than 80 Fireside Elementary fifth graders who had to be rescued by helicopter after being trapped by the flood above Jamestown at the Cal-Wood Education Center. MARK LEFFINGWELL/DAILY CAMERA

# Daily Camera

Bal Swan Children's Center turns 50, Local 1B | Taliban attack kills four, World View 19A

Saturday, September 14, 2013 • $1.00 • www.dailycamera.com

**ONLINE**

www.daily camera.com

• Photo galleries and videos from flooding and rescues
• Full coverage and updates as recovery begins

**STILL UNDER WATER**
Areas of Longmont sifting through floodwaters
Page 13A

**BELLY OF THE BEAST**
Tales from the mouth of Boulder Canyon
Page 12A

**START OF REPAIRS**
Residents take first steps in tackling aftermath
Page 13A

**SPORTS**
• CU postpones football game versus Fresno State, with no make-up date set.
• Flooding washes out all weekend prep events.
Page 1C

# EMERGING FROM THE STORM

The Summit County Rescue team works to save Suzanne Sophocles, center, from her severely flooding home Friday on Streamcrest Drive west of Boulder.
Jeremy Papasso | Daily Camera

## Victims were teen couple returning home with friends

By Sadie Gurman and Yesenia Robles
The Denver Post

Four young friends set off from a birthday party in the craggy hills near northwest Boulder late Wednesday, thunder clapping and rain pummeling their little silver Subaru.

In the driver's seat, Emily Briggs panicked. Water, rocks and mud were rushing down the narrow Linden Drive, slapping against the car and flooding the steep, winding two-lane road.

So 19-year-old Wesley Quinlan took the wheel, and the group — Emily, Wesley, his girlfriend, Wiyanna Nelson, and Nathan Jennings — forged on. But farther down Linden,

See COUPLE, 4A

### Jamestown

## Evacuee: 'The human spirit is alive and well'

### Guard starts evacuating town by helicopter

By Joe Rubino and Mitchell Byars
Camera Staff Writers

After all connecting roads to the small mountain town were washed out by deadly floodwaters and mudslides, rescuers Fri-

day afternoon began the evacuation of the devastated community of Jamestown.

The first National Guard rescue helicopter from Jamestown landed at Boulder Municipal Airport about 2:15 p.m., carrying roughly 20 people and some pets.

Passengers on the twin-engine Chinook checked in with officials, providing

See EVACUEES, 4A

## 172 unaccounted for; 3 dead; federal rescue efforts begin

By Mitchell Byars
Camera Staff Writer

Federal crews began a historic search and rescue effort Friday as 172 people in Boulder County remain "unaccounted for" following 100-year flooding from several days of torrential rainfall.

The death toll rose Friday to at least three after crews found a woman who had been missing since Thursday morning.

Evacuations issued late Thursday for western central Boulder, Eldorado Springs and portions of Longmont remained in effect Friday night.

---

## Right Page (Sunday)

HELTON ANNOUNCES RETIREMENT, Sports 1C

# Daily Camera

Education funds distributed, Local 1B | Ned Mining Museum on upswing, Life & Arts 1D

Sunday, September 15, 2013 • $1.75 • www.dailycamera.com

■ Photos from cleanup and rescue work around county. Page 12A
■ Road damage still being assessed. Page 13A
■ Major reservoirs holding steady, despite week's deluge. Page 14A
■ Businesses slammed as residents deal with damage. Page 15A

Neighbor Birdie Reznickek, right, passes wood to Kate McCarthy, 11, as they clean up a flood-damaged basement Saturday at McCarthy's home on Qualla Drive in Boulder.
Mark Leffingwell | Daily Camera

# Weather provides respite

By Mitchell Byars
Camera Staff Writer

Search and rescue teams on Saturday took full advantage of a break in the torrential rain that has been hammering Boulder County as more than 1,200 people have been evacuated so far in the wake of a 100-year flood in what officials said may be the largest aerial rescue since Hurricane Katrina.

With weather conditions improving, rescue teams were able to send helicopters into the mountain towns of western Boulder County as well as high-clearance vehicles into the town of Lyons to evacuate stranded residents.

"It's been an amazing day, an amazing 24 hours of saving lives,"

See HELICOPTERS, 18A

# 'Amazing day'
## 1,200 evacuated in Boulder County

A woman who asked not to be identified carries her two children while being evacuated by the Juniper Valley Fire crew Saturday on Olde Stage Road in Boulder.
Jeremy Papasso | Daily Camera

# Residents, officials: We will come back

By Joe Rubino
Camera Staff Writer

As residents, crews and emergency responders continue to dig out in the wake of a 100-year flood, state and local officials said they know the road to recovery for Boulder, the county and the rest of Colorado will be a long one.

But, they said, residents will find a way to band together and pull through.

That already was evidenced across the city of Boulder on Saturday. Residents volunteered to help neighbors clean out their homes, build makeshift structures to divert still-receding floodwaters and gather supplies, as many launched what is sure to be arduous recovery in their neighborhoods.

At the same time, businesses offered their support, providing special rates, making donations and hosting

See LEADERS, 17A

## Stranded fifth-graders return to Louisville

### Group was at Cal-Wood near Jamestown

By Alicia Wallace
Camera Staff Writer

LOUISVILLE — The evacuations of people from Boulder County moun-

being stranded at the Cal-Wood Education Center near Jamestown.

The group of Fireside Elementary fifth-graders and 14 adults was airlifted by Chinook helicopters and flown to Boulder Municipal Airport, then bused to the Louisville elementary school at 845 W. Dahlia St., where parents, friends and family awaited.

The group was at Cal-Wood for an

The group had access to shelter, sanitation, heat and food, said Briggs Gamblin, spokesman for the Boulder Valley School District.

Dustin Sagrillo, 34, who was one of the stranded parent volunteers, said he and a group of fathers spent hours shoveling trenches and clearing debris while other parents cooked food and led activities with the children.

"The kids were having fun either

10-year-old closed his eyes, exhaled and gave a big smile.

"I'm so happy," Parker said.

Parker, whose "I went to Cal-Wood with my school" shirt was modified with a marker to say "I survived Cal-Wood with my school," said the experience was not scary and he and classmates were able to do some hiking in the rain.

**Online**
Photo galleries and videos from flooding and rescues
Full coverage and updates as recovery begins www.dailycamera.com

**Weather**
High: 67° | Low: 51°
Showers and thunderstorms.
Complete details on 8C

**TOP LEFT:** Birdie Reznickek, right, passes flood-damaged wood to neighbor Kate McCarthy, 11, as they work to clean up McCarthy's flooded home on Qualla Drive in Boulder on Saturday, Sept. 14. MARK LEFFINGWELL/DAILY CAMERA

**TOP RIGHT:** Colleen Keane looks through a pile of belongings on Sunday, Sept. 15, in Boulder. JEREMY PAPASSO/DAILY CAMERA

**RIGHT:** From left, Steve Gabel and Patrick Muir move a soaked couch out of Muir's apartment on Seventh Street on University Hill in Boulder on Saturday, Sept. 14. Gabel, a neighbor, came to lend a hand. PAUL AIKEN/DAILY CAMERA

**OPPOSITE:** U.S. Postal Service letter carrier Mike Posniewsky looks to deliver mail across a washed out Topaz Drive in Boulder on Saturday Sept. 14. He ultimately scrambled across the debris and made the delivery. PAUL AIKEN/DAILY CAMERA

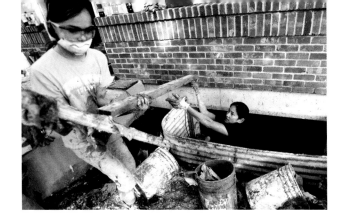

**RIGHT:** Robert Frawley, of Burggraf Disaster Restoration, carries belongings out of a flooded home on Iris Avenue on Sunday, Sept. 15. JEREMY PAPASSO/DAILY CAMERA

**BOTTOM LEFT:** Justin Slyter, with Par Electrical Contractors, looks over fallen power poles at the office complex on Arapahoe Avenue next to Eben G. Fine Park in Boulder on Saturday, Sept. 14. PAUL AIKEN/DAILY CAMERA

**BOTTOM RIGHT:** Evan Russack and his son Trevor, 6, look at the damage to Pennsylvania Avenue on University Hill, which was cut in two by flooding. PAUL AIKEN/DAILY CAMERA

**LEFT:** Wendy Hoffenberg, left, helps Sophia Cornell up to the sidewalk as the rain gets heavy again and the floodwaters begin to rise in Boulder on Sunday, Sept. 15. MARK LEFFINGWELL/DAILY CAMERA

**BELOW:** Tim Eggert, right, places a sandbag as Ed von Bleishert holds down a plastic tarp to reinforce a berm on Seventh Street on University Hill in Boulder. Rain fell heavily again Sunday, Sept. 15, increasing fears of more flooding in the community. PAUL AIKEN/DAILY CAMERA

**ABOVE:** Rocky Mountain Rescue workers Katie Johnson, left, Chris Wentz, Kevin Cossel and Sal Silvester make a game plan before heading out on rescue missions by helicopter on Monday, Sept. 16, at the Boulder Municipal Airport. JEREMY PAPASSO/DAILY CAMERA

**OPPOSITE:** Granger and Suzie Banks walk between discarded and drying household items pulled from a damaged house on Upland Avenue on Sunday, Sept. 15. Rain fell heavily, increasing fears of more flooding in the community. PAUL AIKEN/DAILY CAMERA

**ABOVE:** Trudy Nickola, of Boulder, throws flood-damaged carpet into a massive pile of refuse at the North Boulder Park in Boulder on Wednesday, Sept. 18. JEREMY PAPASSO/DAILY CAMERA

**OPPOSITE:** Adan Zepeda, of Overtime Landscaping, discards damaged belongings from a unit in the Manhattan West Apartments on Wednesday, Sept. 18. JEREMY PAPASSO/DAILY CAMERA

**BELOW:** City of Boulder Storm Utilities Maintenance worker Mike Lozana cleans debris from a storm drain on Wednesday, Sept. 18. JEREMY PAPASSO/DAILY CAMERA

# Daily Camera

City Council to tackle flood agenda, Local 1B | Navy Yard gunman kills 12, World View 4A

Tuesday, September 17, 2013 • $1.00 • www.dailycamera.com

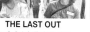

**THE LAST OUT**
Lyons family stuck without water, power
Page 7A

**RAINY RECORD**
City breaks its annual rainfall record
Page 8A

**WADING THROUGH**
Longmont still soaked by floodwaters
Page 1B

For more photos and videos from the past week's flooding: dailycamera.com

Jeremy Papasso | Daily Camera

Evacuees hurry across the tarmac at the Boulder Municipal Airport after being rescued by helicopter from the Pinewood Springs area on Monday.

# DESTROYED

## AT LEAST 119 BOULDER COUNTY HOMES GONE

**By Ashley Dean**
Camera Staff Writer

Boulder County late Monday revealed the first hint of the extent of property damage wrought by last week's historic 100-year flood, announcing that, so far, officials have confirmed 119 homes were destroyed by rampaging floodwaters and mudslides, while another 111 were damaged — numbers that surely will rise in the coming days and weeks.

Additionally, one commercial building was confirmed destroyed and 28 more damaged.

That news followed Monday's successful resumption of the Boulder airlift, with helicopters from the Colorado National Guard — aided by the end to nearly a week's worth of rain — ferrying trapped residents out of the foothills back to Boulder Municipal Airport.

By 9:45 p.m., the Boulder Office of Emergency Management

*See COMMUNITY, 12A*

## 'Boots on the ground'

FEMA sends rescue teams into flooded areas

**By Mitchell Byars**
Camera Staff Writer

As rain continued to come down at Boulder Municipal Airport early Monday morning, six 10-man Federal Emergency Man-

## Boulder taking steps to reopen

City returns to some normalcy as shops, CU re-open doors

**By Sarah Kuta and Brittany Anas**
Camera Staff Writers

Baristas bustled behind the counter of The Cup on Pearl Street while customers filled nearly every seat and table inside the Boulder coffee shop Monday afternoon.

Residents sipped lattes, typed away on laptops and enjoyed a welcome sight — the sun — outside on the restaurant's front patio.

"People were screaming for just a place to hang out and change their scenery and talk about their stories with other people, just kind of vent it through," said co-owner Wendy Ball.

Boulder emerged from days of flooding, returning to some normalcy on Monday, as the University of Colorado resumed classes, downtown businesses kept regular hours and city libraries and

*See OPENINGS, 12A*

### Lyons

## Officials: 'Stay out of town'

Public safety biggest concern

**By Quentin Young**
Longmont Times-Call

Public safety is the biggest concern of officials in Lyons, where massive flooding has wiped out virtually all utilities.

The message from town administrator Victoria Simonsen on Monday was: "Stay out of town."

Flooding shut down Lyons' water, wastewater, electric and gas services, and it could be months before they are restored, town officials said. This creates a hazard for people who remain in town.

"We have major concerns for public health and safety," said Simonsen, who led a media tour of Lyons on Monday afternoon.

The town had no known

*See STRUCTURES, 12A*

### Weather

**High: 81°** | **Low: 54°**

Partly to mostly sunny.
Complete details on 9C

**ABOVE:** Will Vandenberge waits with his daughter, Mia, 4, on Thursday, Sept. 19, outside the disaster center the city of Boulder and Boulder County opened at 5495 Arapahoe Ave. in Boulder. This center, along with another Disaster Assistance Center in Longmont, was open to any Boulder County resident impacted by the flood. CLIFF GRASSMICK/DAILY CAMERA

**LEFT:** Bejamin Nelson, his mother Jennifer and father Ron look at the portrait of their sister and daughter, Wiyanna Nelson, during the memorial service for Wiyanna and Wesley Quinlan at NCAR in Boulder on Saturday, Sept. 21. The teenagers were killed trying to escape the floodwaters in Boulder. CLIFF GRASSMICK/DAILY CAMERA

**BOTTOM LEFT:** Mourners comfort each other after the memorial service for Nelson and Quinlan on Saturday, Sept. 21. CLIFF GRASSMICK/DAILY CAMERA

**BOTTOM MIDDLE:** Glenda Aretxuloeta, mother of Wesley Quinlan, becomes emotional while looking at photos of her son and Nelson during the memorial service for the couple. CLIFF GRASSMICK/DAILY CAMERA

**BOTTOM RIGHT:** Friends and family conduct a Native American directional prayer at the beginning of the memorial service for Nelson and Quinlan at NCAR. CLIFF GRASSMICK/DAILY CAMERA

**ABOVE:** Ben Boyer, coach of the Boulder High School Mountain Bike Team, smiles with his arms in the air after the team presented him with a new mountain bike at Boulder High on Thursday, Oct. 3. The team's bicycles, along with Boyer's bike, were stolen from their storage trailer during the floods. Boyer purchased replacement bicycles for the kids who didn't have them, but he didn't have enough money to replace his own bike. So the team stepped in and held a fundraiser to buy Boyer a new bike.
MARK LEFFINGWELL/DAILY CAMERA

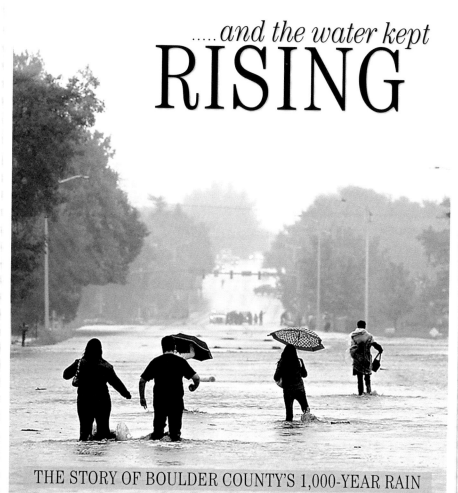

# Daily Camera

Sunday, September 22, 2013 • $1.75 • www.dailycamera.com

## .....and the water kept
# RISING

## THE STORY OF BOULDER COUNTY'S 1,000-YEAR RAIN

By Charlie Brennan and John Aguilar • Camera Staff Writers

The talk on the street the first full weekend of September was about the heat. Boulder tied a record for the date with 93 degrees that Sunday.

At Folsom Field the night of Sept. 7, as the University of Colorado football team claimed its first home win in two years, many Buffs fans wore shorts, light shirts and flip-flops, and not much else.

The experts said the late-summer bake was going to ease. They talked about a cold front in the forecast for Monday, Sept. 9, likely to break the September simmer. And forecasters were looking at an unusually high level of moisture in the atmosphere. Some much-needed rain was on the horizon.

Monday dawned as one more beautiful late-summer day. But clouds began to build over the foothills by midday.

Late in the afternoon, the rain started coming down.

There was no way to know the region was in the first hours of what experts would ultimately call a 1,000-year rain and a 100-year flood.

**LEFT:** Heather Knierim carefully organizes photos that were damaged in September's floods, while trying to clean them up at her home in Boulder on Wednesday, Oct. 9. Knierim, Meg Blum and Diana Ewing have been helping clean photos for people who were hit hard by the flooding.
MARK LEFFINGWELL/DAILY CAMERA

**BOTTOM LEFT:** The Fray perform at the Colorado Rising Concert to benefit Colorado flood victims on Sunday, Oct. 27
CLIFF GRASSMICK/DAILY CAMERA

**BOTTOM RIGHT:** Dave Matthews performs at the Colorado Rising Concert at the 1ST Bank Center in Broomfield on Sunday, Oct. 27, in a benefit for flood victims.
CLIFF GRASSMICK/DAILY CAMERA

# CHAPTER TWO

# Longmont

**The morning of Sept. 12, as the St. Vrain River swelled to** its flooded crest, Longmont residents traveling Hover Street abandoned cars and started wading, desperate to reach the north side of the city. Rain dropped relentlessly on an already-soaked landscape, and a couple of those people — up to their knees in water — still carried their umbrellas.

The image, captured by photographer Lewis Geyer, will endure.

Hover crosses the river just south of Third Avenue and is one of the city's north-south arterials. It carries thousands of cars per day, at 45 mph.

Not that day.

A mile wide at one point, the St. Vrain River covered, closed or wiped out all but one north-south connection from 75th Street to Weld County Road 1. Farther east of the city, the St. Vrain compromised the Colo. 119 bridge and ripped through WCR 13 near Firestone. Water flooded intersections and isolated Carbon Valley neighborhoods. A sea rolled over southwest Weld County.

Yet on that day, and in days that followed, other images emerged, other stories surfaced. The torrent that cut communities in two brought neighbors and strangers together. Volunteers mobilized to clean flooded homes, supply and shelter those who had lost everything, and feed those who tirelessly worked. Longmont and Carbon Valley residents discovered their heroes.

Those images — of mud-covered volunteers, of hugs and smiles — will endure as signs of a community that emerged from this disaster strong, thankful and holding tightly to the ties that unite us.

---

**LEFT:** Longmont residents trying to get to the north side of the city walk north on a flooded Hover Street on Thursday, Sept. 12. LEWIS GEYER/LONGMONT TIMES-CALL

**TOP LEFT:** A sign posted to a barricade is nearly submerged by the St. Vrain River on Thursday, Sept. 12, in Longmont.
MATTHEW JONAS/LONGMONT TIMES-CALL

**TOP RIGHT:** Ella Johnson, 12, loads her puppy Virginia into her car as her family evacuates their South Bowen Street home at 9:45 a.m. on Thursday, Sept. 12.
LEWIS GEYER/LONGMONT TIMES-CALL

**RIGHT:** A Longmont police car drives through a flooded parking lot adjacent to a flooded Warren Avenue near South Main Street on Thursday, Sept. 12.
LEWIS GEYER/LONGMONT TIMES-CALL

**LEFT:** Separated from his pickup by flooding along Price Road at Boston Avenue, Don Potter stands on the washed out railroad track at noon Thursday, Sept. 12. LEWIS GEYER/LONGMONT TIMES-CALL

**BELOW:** A man sits trapped in his pickup, while another man watches from the roof of W.P Manufacturing at Price Road and Boston Avenue at noon Thursday Sept. 12. Eventually the trapped man was able to move his pickup closer to the building and walk inside. LEWIS GEYER/LONGMONT TIMES-CALL

**LEFT:** A man stands on a pickup outside AP Automotive along Price Road on Thursday, Sept. 12. He was later rescued by Longmont firefighters in a large forklift. LEWIS GEYER/LONGMONT TIMES-CALL

**OPPOSITE:** Alberto, no last name given, center, Laura Hughes, of Hygiene, left, and Boulder County Sheriff's Deputy Mitchell Rosebrough work to free a pair of horses from floodwaters near Hygiene Road and North 75th Street on Thursday, Sept. 12, near Hygiene. MATTHEW JONAS/LONGMONT TIMES-CALL

**BOTTOM LEFT:** Logan Goodner, 16, of Longmont, crosses Airport Road near Mountain View Avenue on Thursday, Sept. 12, in Longmont. MATTHEW JONAS/LONGMONT TIMES-CALL

**BOTTOM RIGHT:** Floodwaters surround a road sign near South Pratt Parkway at 7 a.m. Friday, Sept. 13. LEWIS GEYER/LONGMONT TIMES-CALL

**ABOVE:** Cathy and Danny Hirsch make their way across a flooded Boston Avenue at Hover Street on Thursday, Sept. 12. LEWIS GEYER/LONGMONT TIMES-CALL

**OPPOSITE:** A woman takes photos of a guardrail and flood damage on Weld County Road 1 on Friday, Sept. 13, near Longmont. MATTHEW JONAS/LONGMONT TIMES-CALL

**BELOW:** Insects cling to a fence to avoid the rushing water near Airport Road on Thursday, Sept. 12, in Longmont. MATTHEW JONAS/LONGMONT TIMES-CALL

TimesCall.com/Social-Media/

# TIMES-CALL

Rain showers
High 73, Low 52
Details on B6

$1.00  FRIDAY, SEPTEMBER 13, 2013 · No. 256 · LONGMONT, COLORADO

# The Flood

## 500-year deluge nearly cuts Longmont in two, forces evacuations across the Front Range

By Tony Kindelspire and Scott Rochat
Longmont Times-Call

LONGMONT — Longmont's city manager declared a state of emergency Thursday morning as the rapidly rising St. Vrain River and Left Hand Creek effectively cut the city in two.

The rising waters, declared a "500-year flood" by city officials, forced neighborhoods to evacuate and major streets to close, including major north-south routes such as Main Street, Hover Street, Sunset Street and Airport Road. Police and city crews spanned the south side of Longmont to warn residents and redirect traffic, reporting the conditions they found to the city's emergency command center, which city officials activated at 2:30 a.m. Later in the day, as the waters continued to rise, neighborhoods just east of Airport Road near Twin Peaks Golf Course were evacuated.

The blocked and flooded streets drove some to frustration as they tried to find a way across the swollen rivers. At Hover Street and

Please see LONGMONT, on A6

Separated from his pickup due to flooding along Price Road at Boston Avenue, Don Potter stands on the washed-out railroad track at around noon Thursday. To see more photos and a video from Thursday, visit www.TimesCall.com. Lewis Geyer / Times-Call

### BOULDER COUNTY

## 'We are still in life-safety mode'

**President Barack Obama OKs federal disaster aid**

By Brittany Anas
For the Times-Call

BOULDER — President

flooding that has, so far, resulted in two confirmed deaths, at least nine more missing and National Guard rescue efforts.

Continued flooding caused dozens more evacuations throughout the county, power outages and the closure of U.S. Highway 36 on Thursday. Parts

## Flooding carves up Lyons

**Residents: Town divided into 'islands'**

By Quentin Young
Longmont Times-Call

Much of the town of Lyons was submerged Thursday after the St. Vrain River spilled over its banks and barreled through neighborhoods.

Lyons is "facing a 500-year flood event," the town said on its Facebook page Thursday.

The South St. Vrain River roars through Lyons on Thursday. Kenneth Wajda / Courtesy photo

### Inside
35 homes evacuated in Frederick, Firestone **A3**
Officials: Flood is 500-year event **A3**
St. Vrain closed today; many challenges ahead for district **A3**
Longmont water system, wastewater plant shut down **A6**
Where to go for help **A7**

### To our readers:
Due to the extreme weather, some deliveries might be delayed or simply impossible.
We apologize for the inconvenience and appreciate your

**LEFT:** Kim Rapp of Longmont takes photos of the flooded St. Vrain River from the Martin Street bridge Friday, Sept. 13, in Longmont.
MATTHEW JONAS/LONGMONT TIMES-CALL

**OPPOSITE:** Water flows underneath the South Pratt Parkway bridge over the railroad tracks, looking east down First Avenue at 7 a.m. Friday, Sept. 13.
LEWIS GEYER/LONGMONT TIMES-CALL

**BOTTOM LEFT:** Damage at Pella Crossing near Hygiene is seen Saturday, Sept. 14, outside Longmont.
MATTHEW JONAS/LONGMONT TIMES-CALL

**BOTTOM RIGHT:** A once buried utility line is exposed by floodwaters at Pella Crossing on Saturday, Sept. 14, near Hygiene.
MATTHEW JONAS/LONGMONT TIMES-CALL

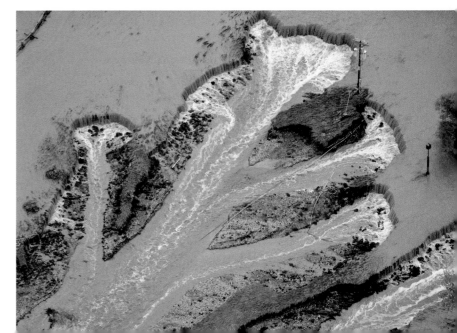

**TOP RIGHT:** Janice Wheeler cries as she greets her son Nathan Wheeler at LifeBridge Church on Friday morning, Sept. 13, after Nathan was evacuated from Lyons. LEWIS GEYER/LONGMONT TIMES-CALL

**ABOVE:** A horse stands next to a shed surrounded by water along Fordham Street on Saturday afternoon, Sept. 14. The horse's owner did not evacuate and was able to take care of it. LEWIS GEYER/LONGMONT TIMES-CALL

**TOP LEFT:** Longmont animal control officer Diane Milford carries a cat taken from an evacuated home across a flooded Hayden Court on Saturday afternoon, Sept. 14. LEWIS GEYER/LONGMONT TIMES-CALL

**LEFT:** Rachel Ferguson, right, hugs an acquaintance in front of the home at 108 Gay St., in the Bohn Park neighborhood, Saturday morning, Sept. 14. Ferguson, a friend of the home's residents, was helping with cleanup. LEWIS GEYER/LONGMONT TIMES-CALL

**ABOVE:** Sonny Stratton, 67, surveys the damage to his business, Sonny's Garage, 108 Gay St., on Saturday morning, Sept. 14. Stratton opened the repair shop in 1976. "It's a mess, looks like I'll probably be gone. We'll see, it's not good," Stratton said. LEWIS GEYER/LONGMONT TIMES-CALL

**ABOVE:** Longmont resident Kristin McDonald and her dog Sakari quickly evacuate their home after a notice from the city that conditions up stream had changed, Sunday, Sept. 15, in Longmont. MATTHEW JONAS/LONGMONT TIMES-CALL

**LEFT:** A damaged bridge on Weld County Road 1 is seen Saturday, Sept. 14, outside of Longmont.
MATTHEW JONAS/LONGMONT TIMES-CALL

**BOTTOM LEFT:** Flooding at Pella Crossing is seen Saturday, Sept. 14, near Hygiene.
MATTHEW JONAS/LONGMONT TIMES-CALL

**BOTTOM RIGHT:** A buckled section of railroad track is seen off Twin Peaks Circle on Monday, Sept. 16, in Longmont.
MATTHEW JONAS/LONGMONT TIMES-CALL

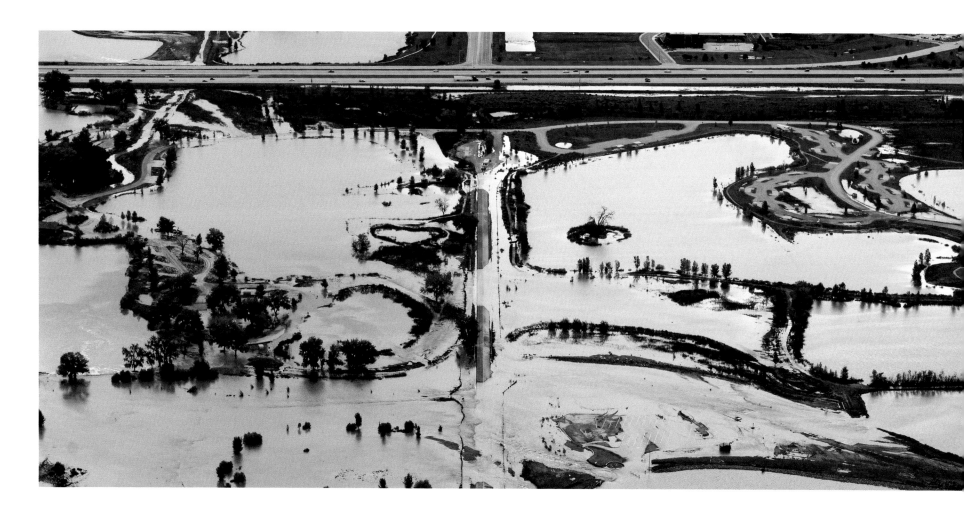

**ABOVE:** Flooding in St. Vrain State Park is seen Saturday, Sept. 14, near Interstate 25 east of Longmont. MATTHEW JONAS/LONGMONT TIMES-CALL

**RIGHT:** The pool at Kanemoto Park is seen damaged Saturday, Sept. 14, in Longmont.
MATTHEW JONAS/LONGMONT TIMES-CALL

# TIMES-CALL

More rain possible
High 77, Low 54
Details on B11

$1.00    SATURDAY, SEPTEMBER 14, 2013 · No. 257 · LONGMONT, COLORADO

## Some city neighborhoods reopen

### But other areas still flooded; 1,300 of 7,200 evacuated households allowed back in

By Tony Kindelspire
Longmont Times-Call

LONGMONT — The day after a 24 hours that no one around here will ever forget, 18 percent of the 7,200 households that were evacuated in Longmont were allowed to return to their homes Friday. About 1,300 households in the Willow Creek and Renaissance neighborhoods in the southwest corner of town were allowed back in, with the understanding they would be subject to re-evacuation should weather conditions change and the flooding in the city worsen.

That's good news for them, but the news for the remaining 5,900 households is not so good. Those neighborhoods that remain evacuated are that way because they have either been flooded to some extent or are in great danger of becoming so, according to city emergency manager Dan Eamon. He estimated that the earliest that people in those neighborhoods will be let back in is Monday, and that's if the weather doesn't turn nasty, which it is supposed to do, again, this weekend.

The National Weather Service is calling for only a

Please see CITY, page A5

### A town unmoved

#### Lyons residents bind together in face of flood

By Greg Lindstrom
Longmont Times-Call

LYONS — In the early hours of Thursday morning, after they had abandoned their homes and headed uphill to the elementary school, the 125 or so evacuees formulated a plan for saving their community.

They assembled a team of doctors and nurses from the group and set up a triage center in Lyons Elementary School's principal's office. They disassembled the gym, pulling down mats and finding anything soft to sleep on. The rest of that morning, as floodwaters rose and then roared down the middle of town, more than 150 people stayed at the school.

The evacuees ranged in age from 2 weeks to 94 years, said evacuee Peter Watson, himself somewhere toward the middle of that span. Many cats and dogs were brought to the school, too.

Residents pitched in whatever they could, bringing with them blankets, clothing, food and other supplies.

Alyssa Frideres, who helped organize the evacuation center at Lyons Elementary School, said the Lyons residents provided everything for one another until the Colorado National Guard brought cots late Thursday evening.

Tanya Daty, who with Peterson and Frideres started the organization of evacuees the night the flooding began, said leaders among the evacuees divided the town into seven zones. In each zone, the organizers designated a three-party team that included a medical professional, an emergency responder and a "communication" specialist.

Their job was to see that residents in each zone had someone available to help them.

On Friday afternoon, after the river had retreated enough, townsfolk turned their attention to St. Vrain Market, at the upper end of Main Street. A handful of men gathered to shovel mud out of the store, while women inside collected food.

The market's owner, Neil Sullivan, had done his turn as the main supplier of food for evacuees. He had taken perishables to the evacuation site. Nonperishables are now being doled out to residents who have stayed in the community.

"We're trying to keep it as

Please see LYONS, page A6

> "We're just thankful to have our lives."
> Jim Carstensen of Lyons

414

Left: Gary McCrumb, left, and Jean Ballhorn wade through floodwaters as they carry valuables out of their home, 414 Park Drive in Lyons, on Friday. McCrumb is planning to stay with friends in town. "We're all taking care of each other," he said. Below: Water reaches the roof of some of the structures at Planet Bluegrass in Lyons on Friday. To see more photos, visit www.timescall.com.

Photos by Greg Lindstrom / Times-Call

## All St. Vrain Valley schools closed until Thursday

### District officials working on plan for Lyons students

By Victoria A.F. Camron
Longmont Times-Call

LONGMONT — All St. Vrain Valley School District schools will be closed until at least Thursday, spokesman John Poynton said Friday afternoon.

But schools in Lyons probably will be closed longer.

Superintendent Don Haddad wrote in a letter to parents, "We are assessing the situation in collaboration with emergency responders and actively developing a plan to continue school for (Lyons) students." More information will be provided over the weekend, he wrote.

board have scheduled a special meeting at 4 p.m. Sunday in the boardroom of the Educational Services Center, 395 S. Pratt Parkway, to discuss the flooding situation.

As the schools are closed, all activities will be canceled as well.

The extended closure could mean that students have to make up days later in the year, but Poynton said figuring that out isn't a priority right now.

**If you go**

**What:** Special meeting of the St. Vrain Valley School District to discuss the flooding and its effect on the schools
**When:** 4 p.m. Sunday
**Where:** Educational Services Center, 395 S. Pratt Parkway, Longmont
**To read superintendent Don Haddad's letter:** Visit http://tinyurl.com/svvsdflood91313.

cided on the extended closure before the weekend, Poynton said, "We believe we're going to need that amined yet.

"We're a long way from having a full assessment of all facilities," Poynton said.

In addition to making sure the schools are safe, district officials have to make sure the roads and bridges used to get students to school are safe, he said.

Although he did not yet have details, Poynton said he knows some schools have been damaged, but

Victoria Camron can be reached at 303-684-5226 or

---

# TIMES-CALL

Storms likely
High 67, Low 51
Details on B12

$1.75    SUNDAY, SEPTEMBER 15, 2013 · No. 258 · LONGMONT, COLORADO

## Longmont is reunited

### City reopens major streets, many neighborhoods

By Scott Rochat
Longmont Times-Call

LONGMONT — A reunited Longmont mostly got to go home again Saturday, though several residents were watching the skies nervously for signs of renewed flooding.

The city lifted most of its evacuation orders throughout the day and also reopened Main Street and Hover Street, allowing north and south Longmont to easily reach each other for the first time since the "500-year flood" hit Thursday. By

Please see REUNITED, on A5

The South Sunset Street bridge over the St. Vrain River lies in shambles Saturday morning.

---

## Longmont evacuees return to homes

### Neighbors rally to clear mud, furniture from flooded homes on Saturday

By Whitney Bryen
Longmont Times-Call

LONGMONT — Piles of mud poured out of Christie Walker's home Saturday as neighbors pushed squeegees across the home's main level, ridding the house of water and dirt brought in by recent flooding.

It was the first time Walker had seen her home, located near First Avenue and Bowen Street in the Bohn Farm neighborhood, since evacuating Thursday morning. Despite the muddied floors and standing water surrounding her house, she was relieved.

"I was imagining that it would be so much worse than this based on the wall of water that was headed this way when I left," Walker said. "I'm just trying to get my grandmother's furniture and some pictures and drawings my son did. Everything else can be replaced."

Evacuation orders were lifted across Longmont on Saturday, allowing most residents back into their homes with the exception of the Champion Greens, Greens and Valley neighborhoods and the area bounded by Secnd Avenue and Spruce Avenue on the north, Ken Pratt Boulevard on the south, Main Street on the east and Hover Street on the west.

At 1311 Ashcroft in Southmoor Park, nine friends gathered to help Jason Kintzer clean out his home.

Please see EVACUEES, on A4

Rachel Ferguson, right, hugs an acquaintance Saturday morning in front of the home in the Bohn Park neighborhood. Ferguson, a friend of the home's residents, was helping with cleanup.

Photos by Lewis Geyer / Times-Call

**Inside**

Customers outside Longmont still without water **A3**

Rescuers retrieve pets for evacuees **A3**

Where to donate **A4**

Where to go for help **A4**

Frederick, Firestone begin cleanup efforts **A5**

1,200 evacuated in Boulder County **A6**

Boulder victims include teen couple **A8**

Sonny Stratton, 67, surveys the damage to his business, Sonny's Garage, 108 Gay St., on Saturday morning. Stratton opened the repair shop 37 years ago. "It's a mess. Looks like I'll probably be gone. We'll see; it's not good," Stratton said.

**To our readers:**

Due to the extreme weather, some deliveries might be delayed or simply impossible. We apologize for the inconvenience and appreciate your understanding.

So that you do not miss today's edition, we have made our online replica edition available for free at http://tinyurl.com/tcedition.

— John Vahlenkamp, managing editor

**RIGHT:** A fully finished basement is seen with standing water at the home of Linda and Ron Rodgers on Sunday, Sept. 15, in Longmont. The Rodgerses were told to evacuate their home after a notice from the city that conditions upstream had changed. MATTHEW JONAS/LONGMONT TIMES-CALL

**BELOW:** Flooded homes are seen near Ninth Avenue by Twin Peaks Golf Course on Saturday, Sept. 14, in Longmont. MATTHEW JONAS/LONGMONT TIMES-CALL

**LEFT:** Floodwaters cover much of the roadway near Dudley Lane and Hayden Court on Saturday, Sept. 14, in Longmont. MATTHEW JONAS/LONGMONT TIMES-CALL

**BOTTOM LEFT:** The flooded neighborhood near Mountain View and Airport Road on Saturday, Sept. 14, in Longmont. MATTHEW JONAS/LONGMONT TIMES-CALL

**BOTTOM RIGHT:** The flooded streets of Wade Road and Hayden Court are seen Saturday, Sept. 14, in Longmont. MATTHEW JONAS/LONGMONT TIMES-CALL

**RIGHT:** A boat is seen tied to a tree off Columbia Drive on Sunday, Sept. 15, in Longmont. MATTHEW JONAS/LONGMONT TIMES-CALL

**BOTTOM LEFT:** People paddle across floodwaters east of Longmont on Saturday, Sept. 14. MATTHEW JONAS/LONGMONT TIMES-CALL

**BOTTOM RIGHT:** A dead fish is seen next to a hose attached to a pump in a basement on Twin Peaks Circle on Monday, Sept. 16. MATTHEW JONAS/LONGMONT TIMES-CALL

**OPPOSITE:** Curt Ingram, owner of Corvette Spa Motorsports, 100 S. Bowen Circle, pushes mud out of his garage Monday morning, Sept. 16. LEWIS GEYER/LONGMONT TIMES-CALL

**SORRY, LITTLE BRO**
Peyton gets best of Eli again as Broncos win
See page B1

TimesCall.com/Social-Media/

# TIMES-CALL

Mostly cloudy
High 74, Low 52
Details on B5

**$1.00** · MONDAY, SEPTEMBER 16, 2013 · No. 259 · LONGMONT, COLORADO

# SUNDAY SCARE

## Another day of rain halts cleanup and leads to new evacuations

By Tony Kindelspire
and Quentin Young
Longmont Times-Call

LONGMONT — Torrential rains on an already drenched city led to more evacuations on Sunday, with some residents having to flee the homes they had started cleaning out on Saturday.

At 5 p.m., the city's Emergency Operations Center issued a mandatory evacuation order for the residential neighborhoods around Third Avenue and Hover Street, including Third Avenue, Bruce Place and Widgeon Drive.

But it wasn't the rain over Longmont that forced residents out of their homes. Weather conditions in the mountains deteriorated early and then continued to get worse through the day Sunday.

For some of the residents it was the second time they've evacuated since flooding began last week. Kristin McDonald and her family were cleaning out their home on Widgeon Drive when the evacuation notice came through. The McDonald home's basement was flooded already, and there were piles of soaked items in the driveway.

"My husband had mementos from a couple generations, and everything's a loss," McDonald said.

She was thankful for all

*Please see SCARE, page A6*

Photos by Matthew Jonas / Times-Call, above; and Cliff Grassmick / For the Times-Call, left
**Above:** Longmont resident Kristin McDonald and her dog Sakari quickly evacuate their home after a notice from the city that conditions upstream had changed Sunday. **Below:** Jay Raymond puts an umbrella over his wife, Margie, at their home near McIntosh Lake on Sunday. They were discussing whether to leave the area or not.

### Inside

- Thousands still without natural gas or electricity. **Page A2**
- Much drinking water must be boiled. **Page A2**
- Thousands await word from more than 300 still unaccounted for. **Page A5**
- Rain stops horses from delivering vital supplies in Larimer. **Page A5**
- Estes Park digs itself out of mud. **Page A7**
- 50 Colorado bridges destroyed or damaged. **Page A7**
- Boulder County activists concerned about flooded oil wells. **Page A10**

## ST. VRAIN VALLEY SCHOOL DISTRICT

# SVVSD faces logistic hurdles

## Lyons students to attend Longmont's Main St. School

By Victoria A.F. Camron
Longmont Times-Call

LONGMONT — Most schools in the St. Vrain Valley School District are expected to be ready to open on Thursday, but Lyons students will have to wait until Sept. 23 to be moved to the Main Street School in Longmont.

The logistics of transporting students and supplying schools were the focus of a special meeting Sunday among Superintendent Don Haddad and other administrators and the Board of Education.

Although school buildings received little damage — mostly water leaks — during the recent flood, district officials have an immense amount of work to do before schools open Thursday. Road closures and damages, as well as power outages, are affecting everything from transportation to school lunches.

"We have to make sure the power grids are all up and running. ... We have to make sure the water supplies are safe," Haddad said.

Because of power failures, most of the food at many schools has spoiled. At the same time — because roads have been closed — the district's warehouse hasn't received deliveries of food, chief operations officer Rick

*Please see SVVSD, page A6*

## Stranded residents told to use flares, sheets, mirrors to alert helicopters

By Brittany Anas,
John Aguilar
and Amy Bounds
For the Times-Call

BOULDER — A major air rescue for the Boulder County foothills devastated by 100-year floodwaters is planned for today, with residents asked to use white sheets, reflective mirrors, flares and signal fires to alert helicopter

### FEMA claims

To make a claim with FEMA, call 800-621-3362 or visit disasterassistance.gov.

copters are on their way, but the county is doing everything it can to get the word out.

A time when the helicopters will start flying hasn't yet been determined, but she said the goal is to take advantage of the clearer weather that's forecast. After a reprieve Saturday from the torrential downpours that had dropped nearly 15 inches of rain on Boulder beginning Monday evening, Sunday's

down the choppers in any way they can."

She said residents should be ready with a bag of medications, clothes and other important items

### To our readers:

Due to the extreme weather, some deliveries might be delayed or simply impossible.

We apologize for the inconvenience and appreciate your understanding.

mile and Fourmile creeks were flooding Sunday afternoon, city of

So that you do not miss today's edition, we have made our online replica edition available for free at http://tinyurl.com/tceedition.

*— John Vahlenkamp, managing editor*

flood also has caused at least $100 million to $150 million in damage

**ABOVE:** The floodwater line is seen on the wall of Lou Belletire's garage on Twin Peaks Circle on Monday, Sept. 16, in Longmont. Belletire had water in both the basement and first floor of his home. MATTHEW JONAS/LONGMONT TIMES-CALL

**OPPOSITE TOP LEFT:** A privately owned M923 troop transport vehicle is partially submerged off Twin Peaks Circle on Monday, Sept. 16, in Longmont. MATTHEW JONAS/LONGMONT TIMES-CALL

**OPPOSITE TOP RIGHT:** The Sunset Street Bridge is washed out Saturday, Sept. 14. MATTHEW JONAS/LONGMONT TIMES-CALL

**OPPOSITE BOTTOM LEFT:** Mobile homes in River Valley Village on Cedar Avenue and Birch Avenue are surrounded by floodwater Tuesday, Sept. 17, in Del Camino. MATTHEW JONAS/LONGMONT TIMES-CALL

**OPPOSITE BOTTOM RIGHT:** Lou Belletire of Longmont looks at his car, which floated into his neighbor's front yard on Twin Peaks Circle on Monday, Sept. 16, in Longmont. MATTHEW JONAS/LONGMONT TIMES-CALL

TimesCall.com/Social-Media/

TIMES-CALL

$1.00     TUESDAY, SEPTEMBER 17, 2013 · No. 260 · LONGMONT, COLORADO

Cloudy with showers
High 84, Low 53
Details on B6

# 'Months to years of recovery'

**Water supply limited; Greenway, pool destroyed; bridges lost**

By Tony Kindelspire
Longmont Times-Call

LONGMONT — City officials on Monday night laid out the scope of destruction left from one of town to the other by the flood of 2013.

"For us, this is going to be months to years of recovery," Dale Rademacher, director of public works and natural resources, said at the State of the City Address at the Civic Center.

Rademacher noted that in the larger, regional context, Longmont had fared better than, for example, its neighbor to the west, Lyons. But Longmont was hardly left unscathed by this natural disaster.

"The National Weather Service has said that this was a rainfall of biblical proportions, and it really was," said

city manager Harold Dominguez, addressing about 75 members of the public and a large contingent of city staffers who came to the meeting.

The daylong rainstorm that began Wednesday had by that night turned into a dangerous situation.

By 2:30 a.m. the city had activated its Emergency Op-

erations Center, and by 11 a.m. Thursday, Dominguez had issued an emergency declaration for the city.

The good news is, as fast as conditions turned from bad to deadly, there have been no deaths or serious injuries in Longmont related to the flood.

The question is where to start with the bad news, but

perhaps water is the appropriate place, since that's what caused all of this devastation.

"The good news is we did a lot of planning," said Dan Eamon, the city's emergency manager, referring to the Lykins Gulch and Left Hand Creek projects, the latter of which was just finished this

Please see RECOVERY, on A8

## Lyons officials: 'Stay out of town'

**Public safety is biggest concern**

By Quentin Young
Longmont Times-Call

Public safety is the biggest concern of officials in Lyons, where massive flooding has wiped out virtually all utilities.

The message from town administrator Victoria Simonsen on Monday was: "Stay out of town."

Flooding shut down Lyons' water, wastewater, electric and gas services, and it could be months before they are restored, town officials said. This creates a hazard for people who remain in town.

"We have major concerns for public health and safety," said Simonsen, who led a media tour of Lyons on Monday afternoon.

The town had no known fatalities as of Monday. It was not clear how many people had chosen to reject a voluntary evacuation notice and stay in Lyons, Simonsen said. Since flooding started last week, administrators began conducting a daily community meeting at 9 a.m. in Sandstone Park. About 500 people showed up Friday.

Matthew Jonas / Times-Call
Part of a historic pavilion is seen destroyed by floodwater in Meadow Park in Lyons on Monday.

Please see LYONS, on A9

## At least 119 Boulder County homes destroyed

A heavily damaged home along the Fourmile Canyon Creek on Lee Hill Drive in Boulder.
Paul Aiken / For the Times-Call

**Officials release first damage figures as airlift resumes into foothills**

By Ashley Dean
For the Times-Call

Boulder County late Monday revealed the first hint of the extent of property damage wrought by last week's historic 100-year flood, announcing that, so far, officials have confirmed 119

homes were destroyed by rampaging floodwaters and mudslides, while another 111 were damaged — numbers that surely will rise in the coming days and weeks.

Additionally, one commercial building was confirmed destroyed and 28 more damaged.

That news followed Monday's successful resumption of the Boulder airlift, with helicopters from the Colorado National Guard — aided by the end to nearly a week's worth of rain — ferrying trapped residents out of the foothills back to Boulder Municipal Airport.

By 9:45 p.m., the Boulder Office of Emergency Management reported that 215 people were evacuated by air Monday, with another 11 rescued by ground. That comes after more than 1,200 were flown and driven out of the Boulder County foothills Saturday during a one-day interruption in the rain.

"Today was a really good day," said Gabrielle Boerkircher, a spokeswoman for Boulder County. "They were able to do a lot of things in the air and on the ground. Tuesday, we'll just go out and do as much as we

Please see COUNTY, on A9

---

TIMES-CALL

$1.00     WEDNESDAY, SEPTEMBER 18, 2013 · No. 261 · LONGMONT, COLORADO

Partly cloudy
High 82, Low 49
Details on B5

# The last evacuees

## Helpers step up in record numbers

By Whitney Bryen
Longmont Times-Call

LONGMONT — Devastation caused by recent flooding has brought together what some are calling the largest mobilization of volunteers ever seen in Longmont.

Hundreds, possibly thousands, of volunteers have stepped up to help their neighbors and surrounding communities after flooding caused damage to hundreds of local homes.

LifeBridge Christian Church is heading up one of the largest volunteer efforts in Longmont, with nearly 1,000 residents on a waiting list to contribute to relief efforts, including running an evacuation center at the church.

"We've never seen anything like this before," said Chris Kouns, volunteer coordinator for LifeBridge. "This is definitely the largest volunteer effort we've ever seen, but it's also the biggest need we've ever seen."

The church is using volunteers to run an evacuation center housed in the church, handling out donations, serving meals and providing information to evacuees.

Within the next week, the church expects to send teams of volunteers into affected neighborhoods to help clean and repair damaged homes, Kouns said.

Neighbors are mobilizing to help clear mud and debris from their communities in affected areas across Longmont.

The city of Longmont solicited volunteers to help with local efforts over the weekend but had to stop taking volunteers after an overwhelming response.

Volunteers from White Fields Community Church helped set up Longmont's disaster-recovery center at Twin Peaks Mall and are offering child care at the Memorial Building evacuation center.

"I'm very impressed with the citizens here in Longmont," said Nick Cady, senior pastor for White Fields Church. "I don't know that this would happen in other places. People here genuinely just want to

> "We've never seen anything like this before."
> **Chris Kouns**
> *LifeBridge Christian Church volunteer coordinator*

Please see HELPERS, page A7

Photos by Lewis Geyer / Times-Call
Agustina Temo, a resident of Royal Mobile Park in Longmont, stands Tuesday in a bedroom of her mobile home, which suffered water damage during last week's flood.

## Royal Mobile Park residents may wait a week to return

By Scott Rochat
Longmont Times-Call

LONGMONT — Broken gas lines. Powerless power lines. Twisted fences and a water-carved chasm to one side of the trailer park's main road.

There's a reason why Royal Mobile Park was the first Longmont neighborhood evacuated Thursday morning in the face of a 500-year flood. And why it's

going to be the last to return. By a long shot.

Not tomorrow. Not the next day. Start thinking a week. At least.

"People can go back in and get their stuff, but it's not safe for anyone to stay," said Longmont Police Cmdr. Jeff Satur.

Come back they have, to salvage what they can, clean what

Please see MOBILE PARK, page A6

### Inside

How to replace vital documents lost to floodwaters. **Page A2**
List of closed roads, parks, facilities. **Page A2**
Del Camino residents check homes despite evacuation order. **Page A3**
County commissioners OK $2.5M in flood-related spending. **Page A3**
Residents allowed back into Lyons for a few hours. **Page A5**
Lyons residents converge on Longmont Post Office. **Page A5**
Some water customers must keep boiling. **Page A5**
Where to go or call for assistance and to pitch in. **Page A7**
Longmont City Council extends state of emergency. **Page A8**
Flood news in brief. **Page A8**

The ground underneath a home was washed away when the flood hit Royal Mobile Park last week.

Royal Mobile Park resident John Minch waits for a FEMA adjuster Tuesday.

# 10 more people rescued; 109 still unaccounted for

By Joe Rubino
and Mitchell Byars
For the Times-Call

At least 262 homes destroyed in Boulder County

Boulder Office of Emergen-

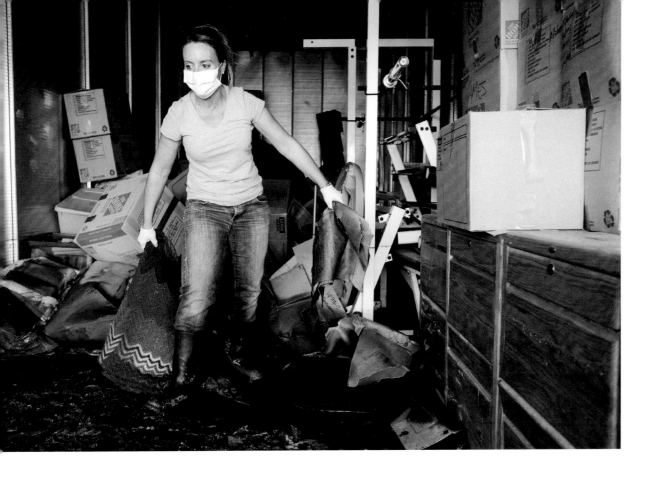

**LEFT:** Amber Genova of Spring Gulch, a neighborhood near Lyons, removes flood-damaged belongings while clearing out her storage unit Monday, Sept. 23, at Storage West Self Storage in Longmont. Genova's home was not damaged by the flood. MATTHEW JONAS/LONGMONT TIMES-CALL

**ABOVE:** Amber Genova of Spring Gulch stands in the mud in her storage unit while sorting belongings Monday, Sept. 23, at Storage West Self Storage in Longmont. MATTHEW JONAS/LONGMONT TIMES-CALL

**BOTTOM LEFT:** Robert Pandolfi of Longmont helps to push water to a pump while working in the basement of Ray Hummer's home on Twin Peaks Circle on Monday, Sept. 16, in Longmont. MATTHEW JONAS/LONGMONT TIMES-CALL

**BOTTOM RIGHT:** John Lee of Longmont points out mold on a violin pulled from a storage unit Monday, Sept. 23, at Storage West Self Storage. MATTHEW JONAS/LONGMONT TIMES-CALL

**TOP LEFT:** A traffic warning sign at First Avenue and Bowen Street in the Bohn Farm Neighborhood is seen with a handwritten high-water line and date marking the flood Tuesday, Sept. 24. MATTHEW JONAS/LONGMONT TIMES-CALL

**TOP MIDDLE:** Flood-damaged photos in a pile outside a storage unit on Monday, Sept. 23, at Storage West Self Storage off Third Avenue and Hover Street in Longmont. MATTHEW JONAS/LONGMONT TIMES-CALL

**TOP RIGHT:** A muddy car seat is seen in a flood-damaged car next to Boston Avenue near the Boulder County Fairgrounds on Wednesday, Sept. 25. MATTHEW JONAS/LONGMONT TIMES-CALL

**RIGHT:** Sharon Kirby-Cole of Longmont talks about her finished basement, which was damaged by floodwaters in her home on the 700 Block of Hayden Court. MATTHEW JONAS/LONGMONT TIMES-CALL

**OPPOSITE:** Rebekah Steers pauses for a moment in her gutted living room on Wednesday, Oct. 9, at her home in Longmont's Bohn Park neighborhood. MATTHEW JONAS/LONGMONT TIMES-CALL

# CHAPTER THREE

# Lyons

**About 2 a.m. Thursday, Sept. 12, Times-Call photographer**

Greg Lindstrom stood on Colo. 66 just east of Lyons. He had arrived moments earlier to find that a Boulder County sheriff's deputy had closed the highway at its intersection with U.S. 36. The St. Vrain River was spilling over the highway, and no one was getting into or out of the town.

The river runs parallel to the highway there, a few hundred feet to the south. Lindstrom heard objects striking the U.S. 36 bridge. The whine of the town's emergency sirens carried through the rain.

It would be Friday morning before anyone from the outside could glimpse the destruction, or hear the amazing tales of how townsfolk escaped rapidly rising flood-waters and pulled together in the predawn hours to save their community.

A convoy of National Guard trucks charged into Lyons that Friday morning to rescue those who had holed up in Lyons Elementary School, which residents had remade into an evacuation center.

Lindstrom talked his way onto a Guard truck heading into town. Hours later, he emerged with the first images of mud-filled homes, tossed and toppled cars, and roads and bridges washed out by a still-raging brown river.

He also brought stories from the earliest hours of the flood, how uphill neighbors took in downhill neighbors, how leaders stepped up to see that help was available to those who needed it most, and how a community came together in the face of "a disaster you wouldn't believe."

---

**LEFT:** Spc. Daniel Lapp, with the Colorado National Guard, drives along Colo. 66 into Lyons as the St. Vrain River rages Friday, Sept. 13. GREG LINDSTROM/LONGMONT TIMES-CALL

**ABOVE:** A destroyed Subaru covered in debris is seen sitting upside-down in the front yard of a home at the corner of Fourth Avenue and Evans Street on Wednesday, Sept. 18, in Lyons. MATTHEW JONAS/LONGMONT TIMES-CALL

**TOP RIGHT:** Lyons residents wave after being evacuated from Lyons on Friday, Sept. 13. GREG LINDSTROM/LONGMONT TIMES-CALL

**TOP LEFT:** The Colorado National Guard is escorted into Lyons on Friday, Sept. 13. GREG LINDSTROM/LONGMONT TIMES-CALL

**LEFT:** Will Wilson is helped into a stretcher as Spc. Daniel Lapp, with the Colorado National Guard, holds an umbrella for Wilson after he was evacuated from Lyons on Friday, Sept. 13. Wilson said a neighbor told him his house was gone. GREG LINDSTROM/LONGMONT TIMES-CALL

**OPPOSITE:** A van sits precariously along the edge of the bridge at Fifth Avenue in Lyons on Friday, Sept. 13. GREG LINDSTROM/LONGMONT TIMES-CALL

**THIS PAGE:** Scenes of the flood damage in Lyons on Friday, Sept. 13.
GREG LINDSTROM/LONGMONT TIMES-CALL

**OPPOSITE:** Residents survey flood damage in Lyons on Friday, Sept. 13.
GREG LINDSTROM/LONGMONT TIMES-CALL

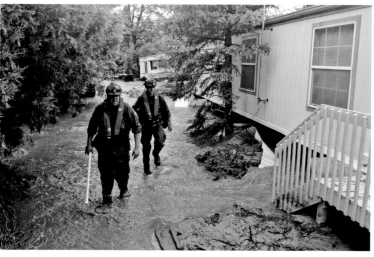

**THIS SPREAD:** Crews from Colorado Task Force Urban Search and Rescue search flooded areas for stranded or missing persons in Lyons on Friday, Sept. 13.
GREG LINDSTROM/LONGMONT TIMES-CALL

**RIGHT:** Gary McCrumb wades through about 6 inches of mud in his home at 414 Park Drive in Lyons on Friday, Sept. 13, as he collects valuables. McCrumb was planning to stay with friends in town. "We're all taking care of each other," said McCrumb. GREG LINDSTROM/LONGMONT TIMES-CALL

**OPPOSITE:** Gary McCrumb, left, and Jean Ballhorn wade through floodwaters as they carry valuables out of their home at 414 Park Drive in Lyons on Friday, Sept. 13. GREG LINDSTROM/LONGMONT TIMES-CALL

**BELOW:** A jeep sits partially submerged in floodwater in Lyons on Friday, Sept. 13. GREG LINDSTROM/LONGMONT TIMES-CALL

**TOP LEFT:** A cow sits on an island as floodwaters rage around it Friday, Sept. 13. Gary Gorman was walking through town with his wife, Karen, and son, Justin, when they noticed their stranded cow. Gorman said it must have washed down at least three-quarters of a mile from his property along Old South St. Vrain Drive.
GREG LINDSTROM/LONGMONT TIMES-CALL

**TOP RIGHT:** Karen Gorman and her husband, Gary, talk about their cow being stranded on an island as floodwaters rage around it on Friday, Sept. 13.
GREG LINDSTROM/LONGMONT TIMES-CALL

**BOTTOM:** Floodwaters erode an area near Colo. 7 outside Lyons on Friday, Sept. 13.
GREG LINDSTROM/LONGMONT TIMES-CALL

**OPPOSITE:** Floodwaters rage along the South St. Vrain River in Lyons on Friday, Sept. 13.
GREG LINDSTROM/LONGMONT TIMES-CALL

**TOP LEFT:** Carmel Ross waves to a helicopter at the Riverbend Mobile Home Park in Lyons on Friday, Sept. 13. GREG LINDSTROM/LONGMONT TIMES-CALL

**TOP RIGHT:** The Riverbend Mobile Home Park in Lyons on Friday, Sept. 13. GREG LINDSTROM/LONGMONT TIMES-CALL

**LEFT:** Flood damage in Lyons, seen from Indian Lookout Road, on Friday, Sept. 13. GREG LINDSTROM/LONGMONT TIMES-CALL

**OPPOSITE:** Ross, a resident of the Riverbend Mobile Home Park in Lyons, walks through the park on Friday, Sept. 13. GREG LINDSTROM/LONGMONT TIMES-CALL

**TOP LEFT AND TOP RIGHT:** Flood damage at The River church in Lyons on Friday, Sept. 13.
GREG LINDSTROM/LONGMONT TIMES-CALL

**RIGHT:** Colorado National Guard Spc. Jose Alvarez inspects flood damage along U.S. 36 north of Lyons on Friday, Sept. 13.
GREG LINDSTROM/LONGMONT TIMES-CALL

**LEFT AND BELOW:** Flood-damaged homes along U.S. 36 north of Lyons on Friday, Sept. 13.

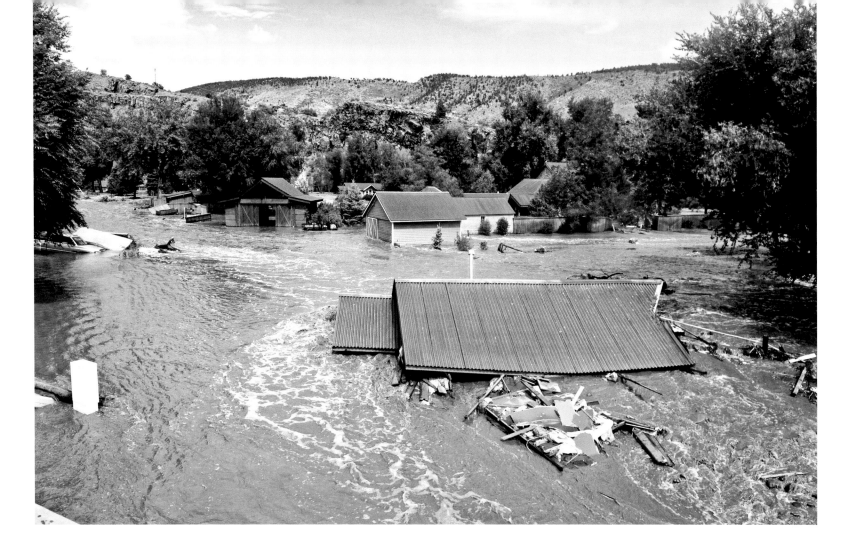

**ABOVE:** Flood damage at Planet Bluegrass in Lyons on Friday, Sept. 13.
GREG LINDSTROM/LONGMONT TIMES-CALL

**RIGHT:** A flooded neighborhood is seen Saturday, Sept. 14, in Lyons.
MATTHEW JONAS/LONGMONT TIMES-CALL

**OPPOSITE** Gary Seifert clears debris from the St. Vrain Market in Lyons on
Friday, Sept. 13. GREG LINDSTROM/LONGMONT TIMES-CALL

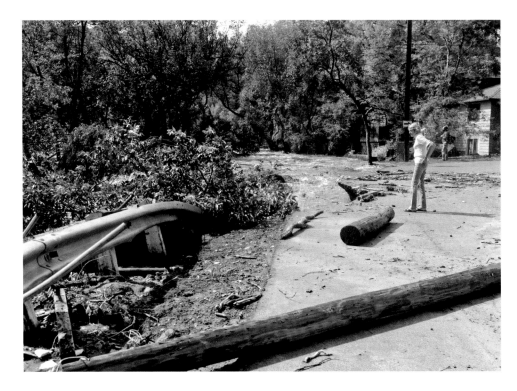

**TOP LEFT:** A fire truck, which appears to be cut off from the road, next to North St. Vrain Creek on Saturday, Sept. 14, near Lyons.
MATTHEW JONAS/LONGMONT TIMES-CALL

**ABOVE:** Homes damaged by floodwaters Saturday, Sept. 14, in Lyons.
MATTHEW JONAS/LONGMONT TIMES-CALL

**TOP RIGHT:** The Lyons wastewater treatment plant is seen Saturday, Sept. 14, in Lyons. MATTHEW JONAS/LONGMONT TIMES-CALL

**RIGHT:** A resident inspects flood damage in Lyons on Friday, Sept. 13.
GREG LINDSTROM/LONGMONT TIMES-CALL

**LEFT:** Floodwaters broke through the underpass along Second Avenue near Bohn Park in Lyons on Friday, Sept. 13.
GREG LINDSTROM/LONGMONT TIMES-CALL

**BOTTOM LEFT:** Flooding from the North St. Vrain Creek damaged North St. Vrain Drive near Lyons.
MATTHEW JONAS/LONGMONT TIMES-CALL

**BOTTOM RIGHT:** A flooded section of Lyons is seen on Saturday, Sept. 14.
MATTHEW JONAS/LONGMONT TIMES-CALL

**ABOVE:** A flooded Park Avenue in Lyons on Friday, Sept. 13. GREG LINDSTROM/LONGMONT TIMES-CALL

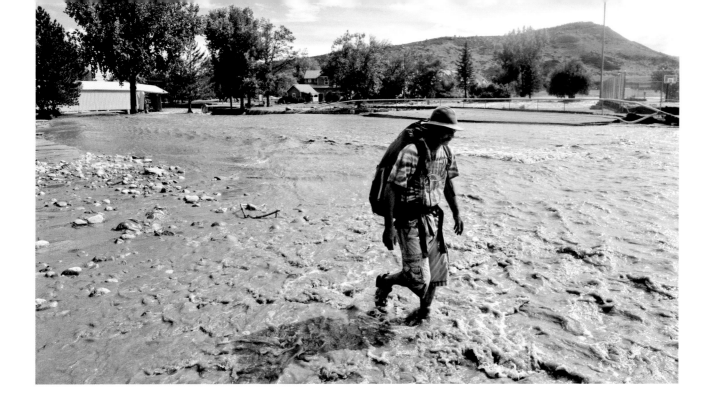

**LEFT:** Chris Melani wades through floodwaters near Bohn Park after coming into town for supplies on Friday, Sept. 13. Melani, who lives up Red Gulch on the southwest side of town, was isolated from the rest of town. GREG LINDSTROM/LONGMONT TIMES-CALL

**BOTTOM LEFT:** Floodwaters consume Planet Bluegrass on Saturday, Sept. 14, in Lyons. MATTHEW JONAS/LONGMONT TIMES-CALL

**BOTTOM RIGHT:** A home appears to have escaped the brunt of floodwaters along Second Avenue near Bohn Park in Lyons. GREG LINDSTROM/LONGMONT TIMES-CALL

**ABOVE:** A Colorado National Guard Chinook helicopter evacuates residents near Lyons on Saturday, Sept. 14. MATTHEW JONAS/LONGMONT TIMES-CALL

**LEFT:** Streets filled with mud and debris and a garage that appears to be leaning are seen Wednesday, Sept. 18, in Lyons. MATTHEW JONAS/LONGMONT TIMES-CALL

**OPPOSITE:** A house that appears undamaged next to North St. Vrain Creek on Saturday, Sept. 14, in Lyons. MATTHEW JONAS/LONGMONT TIMES-CALL

**LEFT:** Cynthia Cappel of Lyons shovels mud and debris out of the basement of her house Wednesday, Sept. 18, near the St. Vrain River. MATTHEW JONAS/LONGMONT TIMES-CALL

**BOTTOM LEFT:** A doll is stuck in a white picket fence near a home that is surrounded by mud and debris Wednesday, Sept. 18, in Lyons. MATTHEW JONAS/LONGMONT TIMES-CALL

**BOTTOM MIDDLE:** Mud and debris fill the wheelwell of a pickup truck on Wednesday, Sept. 18, in Lyons. MATTHEW JONAS/LONGMONT TIMES-CALL

**BOTTOM RIGHT:** A road-closed sign blocks one lane of the Fifth Avenue bridge near Evans Street on Wednesday, Sept. 18, in Lyons. MATTHEW JONAS/LONGMONT TIMES-CALL

**OPPOSITE:** A scooter is partially submerged in mud on Evans Street on Wednesday, Sept. 18, in Lyons. MATTHEW JONAS/LONGMONT TIMES-CALL

# CHAPTER FOUR

# Mountain Towns

**When the river rises, the axiom is to seek higher ground.**

But higher elevation did little to help those living in mountain communities west of Boulder, where deep-cut canyons quickly became conduits of raging torrents.

The canyons filled not only with a deluge of water, but all manner of deadly debris, from trees to boulders to propane tanks to vehicles to houses. In Jamestown, Little James Creek transformed in what seemed an instant into a rushing river five times its normal width and many times its normal speed.

Joseph Howlett, 72, former owner of the Jamestown Mercantile, was killed on Thursday, Sept. 12, when his home collapsed on him after it was pummeled by rushing waters.

Jamestown became cut off to the east, with portions of Lefthand Canyon and James Canyon drives rendered impassible by collapsed roadbed, stranded boulders and mudslides. After the flood receded, helicopters piloted by members of the National Guard swooped over the carnage to ferry residents to safety.

The emergency pickups included the evacuation of more than 80 fifth-graders from Louisville's Fireside Elementary School and their chaperones, isolated at Cal-Wood Education Center, up the mountain from Jamestown, while on an outing to learn about the less-brutal aspects of nature.

A little farther to the south, communities such as Salina that had endured one of the then-worst wildfires in the state's history just three years earlier were now doing battle against another of Mother Nature's terrifying forces. In one foothills canyon after another, debris-choked creeks carried pieces of peoples' lives downstream.

"There was a canyon where the road used to be," Four Mile Fire Chief Bret Gibson said.

---

**LEFT:** The Summit County Rescue team works to save Suzanne Sophocles, center, from her severely flooded home on Friday, Sept. 13, on Streamcrest Drive in Boulder.
JEREMY PAPASSO/DAILY CAMERA

**ABOVE:** Suzanne Sophocles, right, hugs Lefthand Fire District's Anne Reid after she was rescued from her severely flooded home on Friday, Sept. 13, on Streamcrest Drive. Sophocles was stranded with no way out of her home. JEREMY PAPASSO/DAILY CAMERA

**RIGHT:** Colin Dinsmore, of Summit County Rescue, center, carries a dog to safety after previously rescuing three people, five dogs and two cats from a flooded home on Friday, Sept. 13, on U.S. 36 near Lefthand Canyon Road. JEREMY PAPASSO/DAILY CAMERA

**BELOW:** An unidentified woman carries two children while being evacuated by the Juniper Valley Fire Crew on Saturday, Sept. 14, on Olde Stage Road. JEREMY PAPASSO/DAILY CAMERA

**ABOVE:** Brian Montgomery helps his mother, Barbara Yanari, clean up the mud in her flooded basement on Saturday, Sept. 14, on Olde Stage Road. JEREMY PAPASSO/DAILY CAMERA

**RIGHT:** Richard Dash evacuates his home on Saturday, Sept. 14, on Olde Stage Road. JEREMY PAPASSO/DAILY CAMERA

**BOTTOM LEFT:** A washed-out stretch of Lefthand Canyon Drive near the intersection of Olde Stage Road on Saturday, Sept. 14. JEREMY PAPASSO/DAILY CAMERA

**BOTTOM RIGHT:** Long stretches of Lefthand Canyon Drive near Olde Stage Road washed away during the flooding. JEREMY PAPASSO/DAILY CAMERA

**OPPOSITE:** Evacuees hurry across the tarmac at the Boulder Municipal Airport after being rescued by helicopter from the Pinewood Springs area on Monday, Sept. 16. JEREMY PAPASSO/DAILY CAMERA

**RIGHT:** Deborah Haynes is directed off the tarmac at Boulder Municipal Airport after being evacuated on a National Guard helicopter from Jamestown, where she had been stranded by the flooding.
MARK LEFFINGWELL/DAILY CAMERA

**BOTTOM LEFT:** Jerrie McBride, right, checks in with authorities after being rescued by helicopter from the Big Elk Meadows area on Monday, Sept. 16.
JEREMY PAPASSO/DAILY CAMERA

**BOTTOM RIGHT:** Evacuees carry their dogs towards an airplane hangar at the Boulder Municipal Airport in Boulder after being rescued by helicopter from Pinewood Springs on Monday, Sept. 16.
JEREMY PAPASSO/DAILY CAMERA

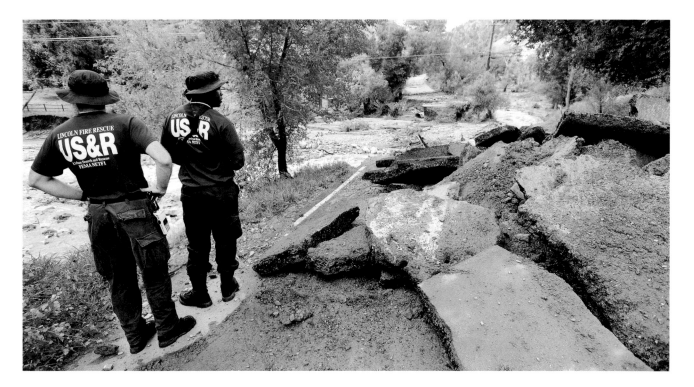

**TOP LEFT:** Members of a FEMA Urban Search and Rescue team and the Colorado National Guard consult a map before checking homes on Lee Hill Drive on Monday, Sept. 16. MARK LEFFINGWELL/DAILY CAMERA

**TOP RIGHT:** A member of a FEMA Urban Search and Rescue team checks homes along Lee Hill Drive to make sure people are accounted for or to determine if they need help on Monday, Sept. 16. MARK LEFFINGWELL/DAILY CAMERA

**LEFT:** FEMA Urban Search and Rescue personnel look over a washed-out bridge and damaged home at the intersection of Wagonwheel Gap Road and Lee Hill Drive. Several homes along the Fourmile Canyon Creek were destroyed or heavily damaged in the flood. PAUL AIKEN/DAILY CAMERA

**TOP RIGHT AND ABOVE:** A heavily damaged home along the Fourmile Canyon Creek on Lee Hill Drive on Monday, Sept. 16. PAUL AIKEN/DAILY CAMERA

**TOP LEFT:** The foundation of this home in Salina was washed away during the flood. JEREMY PAPASSO/DAILY CAMERA

**LEFT:** Keenan Gates walks across a makeshift bridge after assessing the damage to his mother's home on Tuesday, Sept. 17, at the Salina Junction in the Fourmile Canyon area of Boulder County. JEREMY PAPASSO/DAILY CAMERA

**ABOVE:** Local resident Eileen Sharbonda, center, talks with Four Mile Fire Department's Bill Kerwin, left, and Shanti Leasure after being allowed back to her home on Tuesday, Sept. 17, in the Fourmile Canyon area. JEREMY PAPASSO/DAILY CAMERA

**ABOVE:** American Humane Association worker Josh Daniels searches Tuesday, Sept. 17, for a missing cat at a home on Fourmile Canyon Drive that was destroyed by the flood.
JEREMY PAPASSO/DAILY CAMERA

**TOP LEFT:** Staff Sgt. Jose Pantoja is lowered out the door of a helicopter on a rescue mission outside Jamestown, which was hit hard by the flooding.
MARK LEFFINGWELL/DAILY CAMERA

**TOP MIDDLE:** A Black Hawk helicopter rescues people in a mountain area near Lyons on Tuesday, Sept. 17.
MARK LEFFINGWELL/DAILY CAMERA

**TOP RIGHT:** Sgt. First Class Keith Bart helps a woman being winched up to a rescue helicopter near Jamestown on Tuesday, Sept. 17. MARK LEFFINGWELL/DAILY CAMERA

**LEFT:** Staff Sgt. Jose Patoja looks from the open door of a Black Hawk helicopter for people on the ground in need of help near Jamestown on Tuesday, Sept. 17.
MARK LEFFINGWELL/DAILY CAMERA

**ABOVE:** Two women smile and laugh after being rescued near Jamestown on Tuesday, Sept. 17, by a helicopter crew with the 2-4 GSAB 4th Infantry Division based at Fort Carson.
MARK LEFFINGWELL/DAILY CAMERA

**OPPOSITE:** This home near Jamestown was cut in half by the raging floodwaters. MARK LEFFINGWELL/DAILY CAMERA

**LEFT:** Foothills communities near Lyons sustained substantial damage from the flooding. MARK LEFFINGWELL/DAILY CAMERA

**OPPOSITE:** A rescue helicopter from the 2-4 GSAB 4th Infantry Division based at Fort Carson, Colorado, flies a rescue mission over the foothills near Lyons on Tuesday, Sept. 17. MARK LEFFINGWELL/DAILY CAMERA

**BELOW:** A guard rail dips into the creek along a stretch of Boulder Canyon Drive that was damaged by floodwaters. MARK LEFFINGWELL/DAILY CAMERA

**RIGHT:** What's left of a motorcycle and other debris dangles from a tree on Gold Run Road in Boulder County on Thursday, Sept. 19. JEREMY PAPASSO/DAILY CAMERA

**OPPOSITE:** Two men share stories while standing next to a destroyed home on Fourmile Canyon Drive in Salina on Tuesday, Sept. 17. JEREMY PAPASSO/DAILY CAMERA

**BOTTOM LEFT:** Glen Delman of Boulder scrambles across what is left of Gold Run Road in Boulder County on Thursday, Sept. 19. JEREMY PAPASSO/DAILY CAMERA

**BOTTOM RIGHT:** A Salina resident looks at a picture found in the flood debris on Thursday, Sept. 19, along Gold Run Road in Salina. JEREMY PAPASSO/DAILY CAMERA

**LEFT:** Sean McCroskey, left, gets some help from his friend Paul Tagley finding belongings while his wife, Meg McCroskey, watches at their destroyed home in Salina on Thursday, Sept. 19. JEREMY PAPASSO/DAILY CAMERA

**OPPOSITE:** Sean McCroskey pulls his wife's jacket out of the debris in the river in front of their destroyed home on Gold Run Road in Salina. JEREMY PAPASSO/DAILY CAMERA

**BELOW:** Sean McCroskey, right, rolls his bicycle down his roof while gathering belongings from his destroyed home on Gold Run Road. Helping carry belongings from the home on Thursday, Sept. 19, are McCroskey's wife, Meg; family friend Paul Tagley, center; and FEMA inspector Jerry Williams, left. JEREMY PAPASSO/DAILY CAMERA

**LEFT:** Shireen Malik, left, and Bruce Orr help gather belongings from the home of Kathleen McLellan in Salina on Thursday, Sept. 19. JEREMY PAPASSO/DAILY CAMERA

**OPPOSITE:** Salina resident Meg McCroskey walks across a makeshift bridge Thursday, Sept. 19, along a damaged stretch of Gold Run Road in Boulder County. JEREMY PAPASSO/DAILY CAMERA

**BOTTOM LEFT:** Donate Boulder volunteer Juliann Major washes muddy belongings in the creek while cleaning up flood damage at a home in Jamestown on Saturday, Sept. 28. JEREMY PAPASSO/DAILY CAMERA

**BOTTOM RIGHT:** Paul Tagley takes a photograph of his friend's destroyed car on Gold Run Road on Thursday, Sept. 19. JEREMY PAPASSO/DAILY CAMERA

**ABOVE:** This is one of many Jamestown homes that were destroyed in the flooding.
JEREMY PAPASSO/DAILY CAMERA

**LEFT:** Another Jamestown home was knocked from its foundation by the floodwaters.
JEREMY PAPASSO/ DAILY CAMERA

**OPPOSITE:** What's left of a car that was swept up in the flooding sits in floodwater and buried in debris in Jamestown on Saturday, Sept. 28. JEREMY PAPASSO/DAILY CAMERA

**ABOVE:** Southern Baptist Disaster Relief volunteer Steve Winkelman throws flood-damaged drywall into a pile in Jamestown on Saturday, Sept. 28.
JEREMY PAPASSO/DAILY CAMERA

**OPPOSITE:** Donate Boulder volunteers Addy Sage, right, and Theo Merrin work to remove mud and sand from a home in Jamestown on Saturday, Sept. 28.
JEREMY PAPASSO/DAILY CAMERA

**ABOVE:** Southern Baptist Disaster Relief volunteers Stephen Fletcher, left, and Steve Winkelman remove damaged insulation from a home in Jamestown on Saturday, Sept. 28.
JEREMY PAPASSO/DAILY CAMERA

**OPPOSITE:** Salina resident Gurpreet Gill walks thru the debris in a Salina home on Thursday, Oct. 3, that was hit by a mudslide, trapping her and others during the height of the flooding.
JEREMY PAPASSO/DAILY CAMERA

**RIGHT:** Jamestown mayor Tara Schoendinger hugs longtime resident Laura Williams in the flood-ravaged town of Jamestown on Saturday, Sept. 28.
JEREMY PAPASSO/DAILY CAMERA

**LEFT:** Linda Keating and former Jamestown Fire Chief Jim Martella listen to Jim Babcock's eulogy during the Joey Howlett memorial on Saturday, Oct. 19, at the Greenbriar Inn, 8735 N. Foothills Highway.
LEWIS GEYER/LONGMONT TIMES-CALL

**BOTTOM LEFT:** Julie Constantine-Kohlhaas embraces her husband, Matt Kohlhaas, during the Joey Howlett memorial on Saturday, Oct. 19, at the Greenbriar Inn.
LEWIS GEYER/LONGMONT TIMES-CALL

**BOTTOM RIGHT:** Heather Yahnke plays a kazoo, along with most of those in attendance, during the Joey Howlett memorial on Saturday, Oct. 19.
LEWIS GEYER/LONGMONT TIMES-CALL

# CHAPTER FIVE

# Loveland

**For many in the Big Thompson Canyon, the prospect of a** flash flood is never a distant thought.

On July 31, 1976, a torrential storm stalled in the canyon between Loveland and Estes Park, sending down a wall of water that in a few short hours swept away homes and cars. Its speed and power claimed 144 lives, and some victims' bodies were never found. In the flood's aftermath, bridges and roads were engineered to withstand higher water, and many homes were never rebuilt.

As the river rose again Sept. 12-14, 2013, many chose to ride the storm out, believing it would be unable to produce the wall of water seen 37 years earlier.

What they did not know was that the disaster was building far above them, in the highest reaches of Rocky Mountain National Park. As the small streams and creeks converged in Estes Park, their power to destroy was born.

The river became a jackhammer, relentless as it scoured roads to bedrock in many places and destroyed homes, leaving two canyon residents dead in its wake.

More than 1,000 residents became isolated in their mountain retreats. The flood-resistant bridges placed after the 1976 flood remained intact, but the approaches on both sides were lost to the floodwater, rendering them useless. Those stranded had to be rescued by helicopter.

At the mouth of the canyon, the river widened and unleashed its appetite on homes and businesses.

As Reporter-Herald reporter Craig Young wrote on Sept. 29, residents of Loveland will never feel the same way about the rain again.

---

**LEFT:** U.S. 34 at the mouth of the Big Thompson Canyon seen Tuesday, Sept. 17, was ravaged by floodwaters. JENNY SPARKS/LOVELAND REPORTER-HERALD

**RIGHT:** Water in the Big Thompson River rushes past as Mark Smith watches while taking a break from helping a friend move belongings out of the path of floodwater in Loveland on Thursday, Sept. 12.
JENNY SPARKS/LOVELAND REPORTER-HERALD

**BOTTOM LEFT:** Alicia Rowley looks Thursday, Sept. 12, at the much closer waterfront view of the Big Thompson River behind the Waterford Place Apartments in Loveland as the river floods the area. Residents of the complex were evacuated.
JENNY SPARKS/LOVELAND REPORTER-HERALD

**BOTTOM RIGHT:** Youngsters watch for pumpkins floating past in the Big Thompson River just north of Mariana Butte Golf Course on Thursday afternoon, Sept. 12, after heavy rains caused flooding in Loveland.
STEVE STONER/LOVELAND REPORTER-HERALD

**OPPOSITE:** Standing in a flooded field, Bethie Sairob calls to her pregnant goats that are trapped on a patch of land as the Big Thompson River floodwaters rise at River Ranch Goats & Gardens in Loveland on Thursday, Sept. 12.
JENNY SPARKS/LOVELAND REPORTER-HERALD

**ABOVE:** Kalyn Taylor, right, hugs Alexander Diederich and their pug, Phoebe, after they arrived at Timberline Church in Fort Collins on Monday, Sept. 16. Diederich was one of the evacuees rescued from Drake, along with Phoebe. LILIA MUÑOZ/LOVELAND REPORTER-HERALD

**TOP:** The embankment under the BNSF Railway tracks west of Fairgrounds Park gave way early Friday morning, Sept. 13, allowing the Big Thompson River to inundate Railroad Avenue and the park. This picture shows the river at 10:45 a.m. Friday.
CRAIG YOUNG/LOVELAND REPORTER-HERALD

**ABOVE:** A car is submerged in water on a closed Interstate 25 south of Colorado 402 during flooding as emergency personnel block the frontage road on Friday, Sept. 13.
JENNY SPARKS/LOVELAND REPORTER-HERALD

**LEFT:** The Big Thompson River rages under an Interstate 25 bridge south of County Road 20E as Colorado State Patrol troopers block the road Friday, Sept. 13.
JENNY SPARKS/LOVELAND REPORTER-HERALD

**ABOVE:** Quinn Doyle, 5, left, and his sisters, Sofie, 11, center right, and Abby, 10, far right, walk through mud left behind by the flood on Taft Avenue north of First Street in Loveland on Friday, Sept. 13.
JENNY SPARKS/LOVELAND REPORTER-HERALD

**RIGHT:** Stephen Strack checks out the debris and high running water in the Big Thompson River on Taft Avenue in Loveland on Friday, Sept. 13. JENNY SPARKS/LOVELAND REPORTER-HERALD

**OPPOSITE:** A rider on a personal watercraft zips along the water Friday, Sept. 13, on a flooded area where the fairway for hole No. 16 should be at Mariana Butte Golf Course in Loveland.
STEVE STONER/LOVELAND REPORTER-HERALD

**RIGHT:** Adam Small and Natalie Weingardt look across Taft Avenue, which was flooded north of First Street in Loveland on Friday, Sept. 13.
JENNY SPARKS/LOVELAND REPORTER-HERALD

**BOTTOM LEFT:** Pam Robinson, right, a registered nurse volunteer with the American Red Cross, checks on flood evacuee Julissa Garcia, 13, at the shelter in Loveland on Friday, Sept. 13. Julissa was not feeling well.
JENNY SPARKS/LOVELAND REPORTER-HERALD

**BOTTOM RIGHT:** Robert Egloff, left, hugs Sharon Rady on Saturday, Sept. 14, at the Fort Collins-Loveland Municipal Airport where Sharon was picking up her mother, Marge Rady, back, and father, not pictured, who were flown out of Drake where they were stranded by the flooding.
STEVE STONER/LOVELAND REPORTER-HERALD

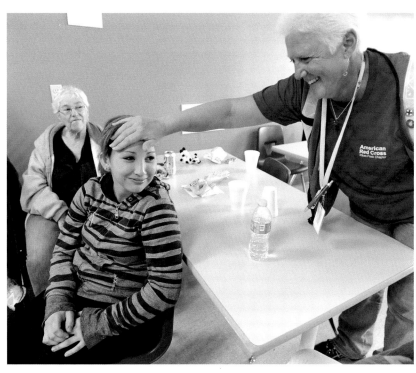

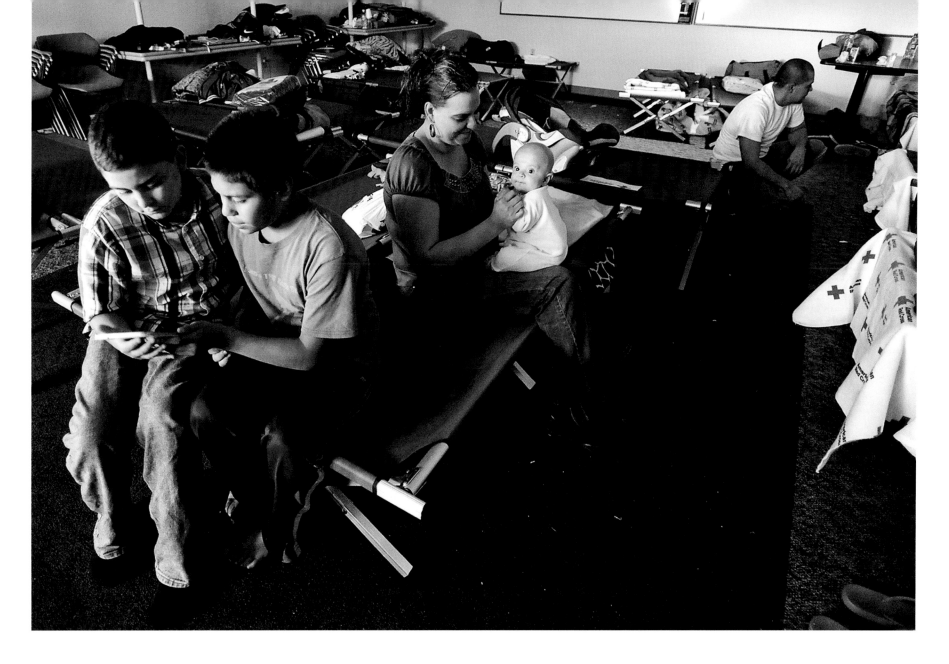

**ABOVE:** Flood evacuee Daisy Velasco plays with her 4-month-old baby, Caleb Bernal, as her nephew Joan Favela, 11, left, and Jesus Jimenez, 12, play a video game at the Red Cross shelter in Loveland on Friday, Sept. 13. Velasco said "not being home" has been difficult. JENNY SPARKS/LOVELAND REPORTER-HERALD

**TOP LEFT:** A Black Hawk helicopter takes off from the Fort Collins-Loveland Municipal Airport on Saturday, Sept. 14, after refueling there before heading out to pick up residents stranded by recent flooding in the area. Seven Colorado Army National Guard helicopters, along with several privately owned helicopters, were used to shuttle people to evacuation shelters.
STEVE STONER/LOVELAND REPORTER-HERALD

**TOP RIGHT:** Haley Yarbrough, 11, rides her bike on the sidewalk on Taft Avenue just north of First Street where mud and debris was deposited along the Centennial Park baseball fields.
STEVE STONER/LOVELAND REPORTER-HERALD

**BELOW:** Peter Williams looks at his neighbor's home, which is standing in floodwaters from the Big Thompson River in the 6700 block of Glade Road on Sunday, Sept. 15, west of Loveland.
JENNY SPARKS/LOVELAND REPORTER-HERALD

LOVELAND • COLORADO

# REPORTER-HERALD

**Saturday**
September 14, 2013

$1.00
ReporterHerald.com

**CANCELED**
Loveland athletics halted
for a spell due to floods

SPORTS, B1

TheRanch
*Celebrating 10 Years*

**CELEBRATION**
The Ranch marks 10 years

INSIDE

## COLORADO FLOODING

### Rocky Mountain National Park closed due to floods

ESTES PARK — Rocky Mountain National Park is closed and visitors have been escorted out of the park because of heavy rain there and flooding in neighboring Estes Park.

Trail Ridge Road through the park, the nation's highest, continuous paved road, remained open to essential travel on Friday.

Superintendent Vaughn Baker said Friday that residents of Estes Park on the park's east side can use the road to evacuate. However, visibility on the road over the Continental Divide is low and drivers need to watch out for debris.

Storms that have knocked out roads and stranded residents have left the park with only limited telephone and Internet access.

Baker says all employees inside the park have been accounted for and some have been evacuated from park housing as a precaution.

— The Associated Press

### Larimer County seeks aid from reconnaissance plane

FORT COLLINS — The Colorado National Guard says it launched four helicopters Friday for reconnaissance and search-and-rescue operations in the Boulder County and Fort Collins areas.

Spokeswoman Cheresa Theiral said the national guard also rescued 104 people on Thursday.

Larimer County Sheriff Justin Smith said Friday his agency is also hoping to get help from a reconnaissance airplane used by the U.S. Forest Service to get the big picture on flood damage.

Smith said telephone service and cell-phone service to Estes Park is down, and ham radio operators are relaying messages to families. He said helicopters will be used to drop food, water and other supplies to people who cannot get to shelters as soon as they can get into the mountains west of Fort Collins.

— The Associated Press

### Flooding closes most of I-25 in northern Colorado

DENVER — Most of Interstate 25 remains closed in northern Colorado.

Southbound lanes of the highway reopened from U.S. Highway 34 to Colorado Highway 402 in the Loveland area Friday evening. But the rest of the highway is closed from the Wyoming border to Colorado Highway 7 north of Denver.

Three major rivers — the Big Thompson, St. Vrain, and the Poudre — normally flow under the highway in northern Colorado, but flood waters have pushed them over the top of the roadway in some locations.

Transportation department spokesman Bob Wilson says the water could weaken the highway.

— The Associated Press

### Today's weather forecast

Couple of
t-storms

**High: 79**
**Low: 55**

# STRANDED

## CLOUDS ARE PARTING, BUT ROAD AHEAD IS LONG

Adam Small and Natalie Weingardt look across Taft Avenue, which Friday was flooded from First Street north to the Big Thompson River bridge.

Reporter-Herald/JENNY SPARKS

### Loveland begins to emerge from flood-imposed isolation

By CRAIG YOUNG
Reporter-Herald Staff Writer

After a second day of battering by the Big Thompson River, cut off from communities around it, the city of Loveland is beginning to see the clouds part.

"The bright spots are that the weather will improve, will begin to dry out," said city spokesman Tom Hacker. "The river is dropping, but it will not drop nearly as fast as it came up."

The river, in a rage not seen since the 1976 Big Thompson flood, had cut every north-south roadway in the city by Thursday night.

Namaqua, Wilson, Taft, Railroad, Lincoln, St. Louis — all were impassable because of the floodwater that started spilling early Thursday morning. Even the railroad link

through town was severed.

When Interstate 25 was closed Friday morning, the only way to Denver was via Greeley and U.S. 85. And then later Friday, even that highway was blocked by the South Platte River.

**FEELING STUCK**

Lovelanders — and everyone else trying to get somewhere on the North Front Range — were feeling stuck.

See FLOOD, PAGE A9

### Officials squash rumors of unsafe water

Some in south Loveland lost service early Friday, but treatment plant is working properly, utility says

By JESSICA MAHER
Reporter-Herald Staff Writer

Some south Loveland water customers lost their service early Friday morning, but rumors of contaminated water or widespread utility shutoffs are unfounded, according to Loveland Water and Power spokeswoman Gretchen Stanford.

On Friday evening, Water and Power crews were still trying to determine the cause of water outages and reduced pressure to customers south of First Street be-

Flood evacuee Daisy Velasco plays with her baby Caleb Bernal, 4 months, at, 11, left, and Jesus Jimenez, 12, play a video game Friday at the Red Cross Shelter in Loveland. Velasco said not being home has been difficult.

Reporter-Herald/JENNY SPARKS

### Residents waiting to return

---

LOVELAND • COLORADO

# REPORTER-HERALD

**Sunday**
September 15, 2013

$1.75
ReporterHerald.com

**FIRST WIN**
Fourth-quarter drive seals
Rams' home opener

SPORTS, B1

**$720**
In coupon
savings

## Helicopters evacuate hundreds of stranded mountain residents to the flatlands

A Black Hawk helicopter takes off from the Fort Collins/Loveland Municipal Airport on Saturday after refueling there before heading out to pick up residents stranded by recent flooding in the area. Seven Colorado Army National Guard along with several privately owned helicopters were used to shuttle people to evacuation shelters.

## COLORADO FLOODING

### Towns near Fort Morgan evacuated by flooding

GREELEY — Some towns near Fort Morgan have been evacuated as flooding spreads across Colorado's Eastern Plains.

Authorities ordered residents of Goodrich, Orchard, Muir Springs and Weldona to leave their homes Saturday.

They're near the South Platte River and three large reservoirs.

— The Associated Press

### Broken line sending raw sewage into Boulder Creek

BOULDER — Boulder is working to address a break in a city sewer main that is allowing raw sewage to enter Boulder Creek.

The city says there's no immediate threat to the drinking water in Boulder or Lafayette, which doesn't come from the creek.

Residents are being urged to restrict water usage on such things as laundry to keep flows into the sewer system to a minimum.

— The Associated Press

### National Guard: 1,200 rescued from flooded areas

DENVER — A National Guard official says airlifts and truck convoys have ferried more than 1,200 stranded residents and their pets from the floodwaters.

Lt. Col. Mitch Utterback said Saturday that more than 500 people were evacuated from Lyons over the past two days using high-clearance vehicles. Another 700 people in the area were rescued by helicopter.

The search-and-rescue operations went on overnight with pilots using night-vision equipment. They were boosted Saturday with at least 12 helicopters participating.

Much of the focus has been on the communities of Lyons and Jamestown. Rescues also are happening to the east as rivers overflow in Larimer and Weld counties.

Boulder County Sheriff Joe Pelle says authorities are making progress in reaching areas previously inaccessible. Hundreds of people in the flooded areas are still unaccounted for.

— The Associated Press

# SURVIVING

By JESSICA MAHER
Reporter-Herald Staff Writer

There was a moment when Drake residents shifted from wondering how bad the storm would be to wondering how they'd survive and when they'd be rescued.

For Marge Rady, it was when she looked out the window.

"We watched our neighbors' homes go right down the river. They're completely gone," she said.

With a duffel bag and a Maltese-Bichon who got more than he bargained for during a dog-sitting trip, Marge and her husband Leroy arrived at the Fort Collins-Loveland Municipal Airport on Saturday afternoon. A Century Link helicopter that had been deployed to examine the data company's lines in the flood-ravaged Big Thompson Canyon rescued them from a home in the Hayden subdivision in Drake.

See FLOOD, PAGE A2

Robert Egloff, left, hugs Sharon Rady on Saturday at the Fort Collins/Loveland Municipal Airport, where Sharon was picking up her mother, Marge Rady, back, and father, not pictured, who were flown out of Drake, where they were stranded by recent flooding.

Reporter-Herald photos/STEVE STONER

## Next step: Recovery

A Disaster Assistance Center will open Sunday at Rocky Mountain Center for Innovation and Technology

By JESSICA MAHER
Reporter-Herald Staff Writer

With a life-safety focus giving way to recovery efforts, Loveland officials on Saturday held the first of what's expected to be a series of meetings for those displaced by the flood.

The meetings, which were open only to those who received evacuation notices because their homes or businesses were situated in the FEMA 100-year flood plain, aimed to open up a dialogue, particularly about the question on everyone's mind: re-entry.

But until the water recedes completely and building and property inspections are complete, Police Chief Luke Hecker said, there's still no definitive timeline.

"We're by no means finished with our operation objectives," he said. "In fact, we're right in the middle of it."

> "While there is some structural damage, it doesn't appear to be significant, especially in the city."
>
> *Police Chief Luke Hecker*

nent re-entry is dependent upon water levels, according to a city news release.

On Thursday, 610 emergency calls went out to people whose homes or businesses are located in the Big Thompson River corridor. But of those, Hecker said, an evaluation on Saturday counted 65 structures that had been built into the flood plain within the city. About 1,000 structures counted in the flood plain are in unincorporated Larimer County.

"While there is some structural damage,

## Floodwaters claim life of Cedar Cove woman

By CRIS TILLER
Reporter-Herald Staff Writer

Law enforcement officials said Saturday that a 60-year-old woman was swept away in the floodwaters of the Big Thompson and is now presumed dead.

The woman, who was not identified, was in the Cedar Cove area in the lower section of the canyon when she was swept away on Friday, according to Larimer County Sheriff's Office Executive Officer Nick Christensen.

Neighbors had heard her home tearing apart because of the rising water, but they were not able to reach her.

"Our hearts and thoughts go out to the family members," Christensen said.

Due to the severity of the conditions in the Big Thompson area, Christensen said he anticipated additional loss of life among

### Today's weather forecast

Rain; watch **High: 63**
for flooding **Low: 48**

Full Forecast on C8

**MORE FLOOD COVERAGE**

**RIGHT:** The Bounds family looks at the destruction from flooding at Glade Park on the Big Thompson River west of Loveland on Sunday, Sept. 15.
JENNY SPARKS/LOVELAND REPORTER-HERALD

**BOTTOM LEFT:** A shed rests in the Big Thompson River as it floods a backyard in the 6700 block of Glade Road on Sunday, Sept. 15.
JENNY SPARKS/LOVELAND REPORTER-HERALD

**BOTTOM MIDDLE:** A destroyed wrought-iron fence at God's Country Cowboy Church is reflected in floodwater in west Loveland on Sunday, Sept. 15.
JENNY SPARKS/LOVELAND REPORTER-HERALD

**BOTTOM RIGHT:** As the Big Thompson River started to flood, the city of Loveland put up warning signs on the Loveland Recreation Trail off Southeast Eighth Street. By Sunday afternoon, Sept. 15, one of those signs had been knocked over by the raging river. In the background sit a boat and shipping containers displaced by the flooding.
CRAIG YOUNG/LOVELAND REPORTER-HERALD

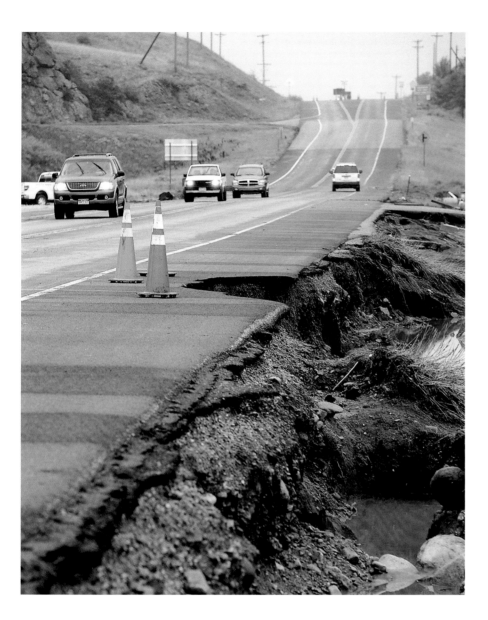

**ABOVE:** Floodwaters washed away part of U.S. 34 east of Glade Road seen here on Sunday, Sept. 15. JENNY SPARKS/LOVELAND REPORTER-HERALD

LOVELAND • COLORADO

Tuesday
September 17, 2013

# REPORTER-HERALD

$1.00
ReporterHerald.com

**SURVEYING DAMAGE**
City Council visits hard-
hit areas of Loveland

FRONT RANGE, A3

**UNDER PRESSURE**
Trio of Loveland golfers
are bound for state

SPORTS, B1

# Clouds lift, rescues begin

Kalyn Taylor, right, hugs Alexander Diederich and their pug Phoebe after they arrived at Timberline Church in Fort Collins on Monday. Diederich was one of the evacuees rescued from Drake along with his dog.
Reporter-Herald/LILIA MUÑOZ

## 260 people remain unaccounted for in Larimer County after Monday evacuations

By ALEX BURNESS
REPORTER-HERALD STAFF WRITER

An estimated 336 people stranded by flooding were evacuated by helicopter Monday to a shelter in Fort Collins, with hundreds more slated to be rescued to-day if weather permits.

Evacuees are being brought to Timberline Church, the same site the Ameri-can Red Cross used as a pop-up shelter

during the High Park fire. An estimated 203 people slept at the church Saturday night, with about 50 expected to do the same on Monday. Most people bused to Timberline either have connected or will connect with friends or family.

Timberline Church, now a massive pop-up donation center for clothing and food, will soon transition donated goods to the

SEE FLOOD, PAGE A2

**Larimer County
by the numbers**

**Fatalities:** 2 presumed dead.
**Unaccounted for:** 260 people.
**Evacuated Monday:** 336 people.
**Helicopters available for rescue:** 16.
**Damaged or destroyed businesses:** 700.
**Damaged or destroyed homes:** 6,000.
**FEMA employees helping with search and rescue:** 160.
**Volunteer hours given at Timberline shelter in Fort Collins:** 5,000.

## Neighborliness springs to action

Glade Road residents
have been helping
each other since
the rain started

By CRAIG YOUNG
REPORTER-HERALD STAFF WRITER

As people along the Big Thompson River begin the long slog of cleaning up after last week's flood, they're learning the meaning of neighborliness.

"Everybody's been helping each other out," said Jim War-ren, a resident of Glade Road who was driving his tractor through the riverside neighbor-hood west of Loveland on Mon-day, looking for people to help.

"It's a great little street," he said.

Warren was scraping mud out of neighbors' driveways Mon-day, and he stopped at a house to pull a stuck car out of the muck.

He said he didn't evacuate during the peak flooding Thurs-day night.

"We stuck it out. We were sandbagging the neighbor's house all night," he said, and building berms that the river promptly overwhelmed.

another neighbor showed up with a load of hay, feed and wa-ter for someone else's animals.
Amie Burton, whose house stands on higher ground, said

Diane Carnahan stands Monday in her sunroom of her Glade Road home which is now filled with mud from the Big Thompson River flooding.
Reporter-Herald/JENNY SPARKS

"They had people driving along here with spaghetti dinners, water, generators. That first day, it relieved so much pressure, knowing there were people to help."

## 13 killed in Washington, D.C., Navy Yard shooting rampage

WASHINGTON — A former Navy man opened fire Monday morning inside a building at the heavily secured Washing-ton Navy Yard, spraying bullets at office workers in the cafeteria and the halls, au-thorities said. Thirteen people were killed, including the gunman.

Authorities said they were looking for a possible second attacker who may have been disguised in an olive-drab military-style uniform.

But as the day wore on and night fell, the rampage increasingly appeared to be the work of a lone gunman, and Navy Yard employees were being released from the complex and children were let out of their locked-down schools.

Investigators said they had not estab-lished a motive for the rampage, which un-folded about 8:20 a.m. in the heart of the nation's capital, less than four miles from the White House and two miles from the Capitol.

It was the deadliest shooting rampage at a U.S.-based military installation since Maj. Nidal Hasan killed 13 people and wounded more than 30 others in 2009 at Fort Hood in Texas. He was convicted last month and sentenced to death.

— The Associated Press

More World news on A6

## Colorado evacuees return to find more heartbreak

Weary Colorado evacuees have begun returning home after days of rain and flooding, but Monday's clearing skies and receding waters revealed only more heart-break: toppled houses, upended vehicles and a stinking layer of muck covering ev-erything.

Rescuers grounded by weekend rains took advantage of the break in the weather to resume searches for people still strand-ed, with 21 helicopters fanning out over the mountainsides and the plains to drop sup-plies and airlift those who need help.

The number of dead and missing people was difficult to pinpoint. State emergency officials reported the death toll at seven Monday, but local officials said it was four, with two women missing and presumed dead.

The number of missing people was drop-ping as the state's count fell Monday from just over 1,200 to about half that. State offi-cials hoped the overall number would con-tinue to drop with rescuers reaching more people and phone service being restored.

—The Associated Press

More Region news on A5

**Today's weather forecast**

Mostly sunny;
warmer

**High:** 85
**Low:** 55

Full forecast on A8

## JUST WEIRD

### Russian shot in quarrel over Kant's philosophy

An argument in southern Russia over philosopher Immanuel Kant, the author of "Critique of Pure Reason," devolved into pure mayhem when one debater shot the other.

A police spokeswoman in Rostov-on Don, Viktoria Safarova, said two men in their 20s were discussing Kant as they stood in line to buy beer at a small store on Sunday. The discussion deteriorated into a fistfight and one participant pulled out a small nonlethal pistol and fired re-peatedly.

It was not clear which of Kant's ideas may have triggered the violence.

— The Associated Press

**RIGHT:** A view of Glade Park with the Big Thompson River running through shows where the parking lot used to be, looking toward the U.S. 34 bridge in west Loveland on Sunday, Sept. 15.
JENNY SPARKS/LOVELAND REPORTER-HERALD

**BOTTOM RIGHT:** What is left of the parking lot at Glade Park after the Big Thompson River washed it away is seen on Sunday, Sept. 15.
JENNY SPARKS/LOVELAND REPORTER-HERALD

**LEFT:** Diana Carnahan stands Monday, Sept. 16, in the sunroom of her Glade Road home, which was filled with mud from the Big Thompson River flooding.
JENNY SPARKS/LOVELAND REPORTER-HERALD

**BOTTOM LEFT:** Diana Carnahan and her husband, Ken, stand surrounded by mud left behind by the flood near their workshop and barn at their Glade Road home Monday, Sept. 16.
JENNY SPARKS/LOVELAND REPORTER-HERALD

**BOTTOM RIGHT:** An antique car is buried in mud and floodwater Sunday, Sept. 15, west of Loveland.
JENNY SPARKS/LOVELAND REPORTER-HERALD

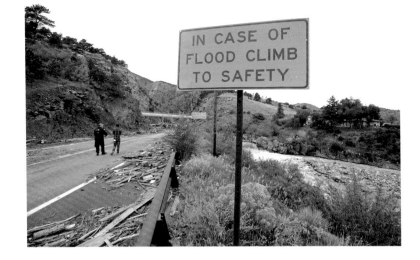

**ABOVE:** Flood damage along U.S. 34 near the mouth of the Big Thompson Canyon is seen Tuesday, Sept. 17. JENNY SPARKS/LOVELAND REPORTER-HERALD

**RIGHT:** Floodwaters tore away chunks of U.S. 34, as seen Tuesday, Sept. 17, west of Loveland. JENNY SPARKS/LOVELAND REPORTER-HERALD

**BELOW:** Floodwater washed away a huge section of Diana and Ken Carnahan's backyard seen here Monday, Sept. 16. JENNY SPARKS/LOVELAND REPORTER-HERALD

**LEFT:** Baricades block off a section of U.S. 34 near the Riverview RV Park west of Loveland on Tuesday, Sept. 17, that was damaged when the Big Thompson River flooded. JENNY SPARKS/LOVELAND REPORTER-HERALD

**BOTTOM LEFT:** U.S. 34 at the mouth of the Big Thompson Canyon, seen Tuesday, Sept. 17, was washed away by the flood. JENNY SPARKS/LOVELAND REPORTER-HERALD

**BOTTOM RIGHT:** A view looking west from the mouth of the Big Thompson Canyon on Tuesday, Sept. 17, shows flood-damaged U.S. 34. JENNY SPARKS/LOVELAND REPORTER-HERALD

**ABOVE:** Joyce Kilmer, right, is comforted Sunday, Sept. 22, by Alice Orrison after speaking about her flood experience during a church service at Allnutt Funeral Chapel in Loveland. Kilmer was forced to leave her friend, Evelyn Starner, as they tried to escape floodwaters in the Big Thompson Canyon on Thursday, Sept. 12. Starner hurt her back and was unable to escape. She was swept away, and her body was recovered several days later. LILIA MUÑOZ/LOVELAND REPORTER-HERALD

**OPPOSITE:** Ryer Porter, left, and Joe Abbatiello, both Colorado State University Air Force ROTC cadets, shovel silt out of the Ketterer's Landscaping workshop Friday, Sept. 20, west of Loveland after the flood. JENNY SPARKS/LOVELAND REPORTER-HERALD

**RIGHT:** Tess Groeneman is framed by what is left of a barn Thursday, Oct. 3, as she uses an air compressor to clean dirt from tools at a home west of Loveland that was hit hard by the flood. Groeneman was part of a team from Resurrection Fellowship church in Loveland that was pitching in to help flood victims. JENNY SPARKS/LOVELAND REPORTER-HERALD

**BOTTOM LEFT:** Standing on the bridge over the Big Thompson River where the road was washed away by floodwaters, David Jessup, co-owner of Sylvan Dale Guest Ranch, talks with a man surveying the damage Thursday, Sept. 26, west of Loveland. The guest ranch sustained heavy damage in the flooding. LILIA MUÑOZ/LOVELAND REPORTER-HERALD

**BOTTOM RIGHT:** Henry Laviolette, right, and his son Elijah, 4, explore an area Tuesday, Oct. 1, near Namaqua Avenue where floodwaters left a ravine more than 7 feet deep. Namaqua Road reopened Oct. 1 after being closed since the flood. JENNY SPARKS/LOVELAND REPORTER-HERALD

**OPPOSITE:** U.S. Sen. Michael Bennet, right, checks out the flood damage on U.S. 34 on Friday, Oct. 6, at the mouth of the Big Thompson Canyon west of Loveland as Colorado Department of Transportation crews work on the road. JENNY SPARKS/LOVELAND REPORTER-HERALD

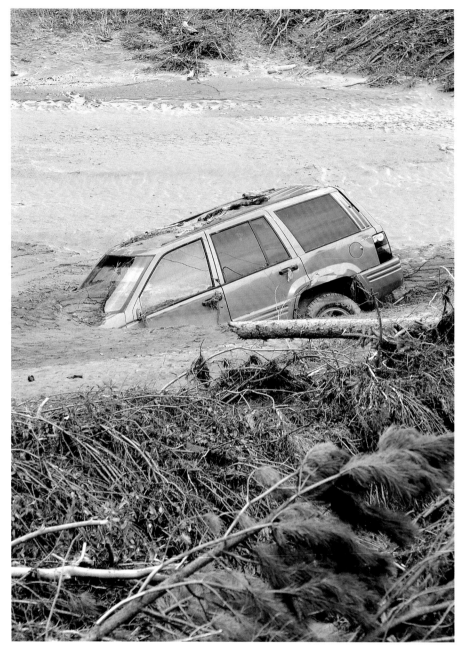

**ABOVE:** Larimer County Commissioner Steve Johnson gets a closer look Monday, Oct. 14, at the flood-damaged Larimer County Road 43 leading into Glen Haven.
JENNY SPARKS/LOVELAND REPORTER-HERALD

**RIGHT:** A vehicle buried by the flood is seen Oct. 14 in Glen Haven.
JENNY SPARKS/LOVELAND REPORTER-HERALD

**ABOVE:** Resident Duke Sumonia walks past the flood-damaged Town Hall and general store Oct. 14 in Glen Haven. JENNY SPARKS/LOVELAND REPORTER-HERALD

**LEFT:** Nick Mishler, left, and Andrew Fierros, in the skid-steer, city of Loveland Parks and Recreation employees, install a fence Thursday, Oct. 17, around the flood-damaged grandstands at Fairgrounds Park in Loveland.
JENNY SPARKS/LOVELAND REPORTER-HERALD

**OPPOSITE:** Dan Willadsen, crew supervisor for city of Loveland Parks and Recreation, shows Thursday, Oct. 17, how the floodwaters ate away at the land at Fairgrounds Park.
JENNY SPARKS/LOVELAND REPORTER-HERALD

**BOTTOM LEFT:** Sidewalks, land and roads were destroyed by the flood, seen here Thursday, Oct. 17, at Fairgrounds Park in Loveland.
JENNY SPARKS/LOVELAND REPORTER-HERALD

**BOTTOM RIGHT:** A sign on one of the bridges that link Fairgrounds Park and Barnes Park, seen Thursday, Oct. 17, warns folks of the flood damage.
JENNY SPARKS/LOVELAND REPORTER-HERALD

**ABOVE:** Val Strals knocks on the door of his flood-ravaged home as he jokes with volunteers, not pictured, as they try to salvage some belongings from his home on Hummigbird Lane west of Loveland on Wednesday, Oct. 23. Strals' home was completely covered with sand and mud from the flood, so he dug into it to see what he could recover. JENNY SPARKS/LOVELAND REPORTER-HERALD

**OPPOSITE:** Federal Emergency Management Agency employee Peggy Smith assesses flood damage at Sylvan Dale Guest Ranch on Wednesday, Oct. 23, west of Loveland with a FEMA crew and Larimer County building inspectors. JENNY SPARKS/LOVELAND REPORTER-HERALD

**RIGHT:** Allen Turner, left, and John Ormsby, Federal Emergency Management Agency employees, walk around a home torn apart by floodwaters on Hummingbird Lane west of Loveland while assessing flood damage Wednesday, Oct. 23, in the area with Larimer County building inspectors.
JENNY SPARKS/LOVELAND REPORTER-HERALD

**BOTTOM LEFT:** Carrie Hayes, left, works Wednesday, Oct. 23, shoveling mud and sand away from her home on Hummingbird Lane west of Loveland. A 1969 Barracuda, her first car, sits buried in the mud in front of her home.
JENNY SPARKS/LOVELAND REPORTER-HERALD

**BOTTOM RIGHT:** A welcome sign hangs Wednesday, Oct. 23, on a home on Hummingbird Lane that is filled nearly to the roof with sand and mud from the flood.
JENNY SPARKS/LOVELAND REPORTER-HERALD

**ABOVE:** Cindy Sprague, left, and Euleta Palser embrace Thursday, Oct. 24, outside the Loveland Public Library as others plant tulip bulbs in honor of Patty Goodwine, who died when her home was swept away by floodwaters. Palser is Goodwine's sister, and Sprague is a longtime friend of Goodwine's and worked with her for more than 30 years at the library. The tulips also were planted in memory of Evelyn Starner, who died in the flood. JENNY SPARKS/LOVELAND REPORTER-HERALD

# CHAPTER SIX

# Estes Park

## There had been several light rain showers earlier in the

week — harmless and typical for an early September in the Rocky Mountains.

Nobody gave it a second thought.

And yet the worst flooding event in Colorado's recorded history was about to unfold along the Front Range as Estes Park residents and others went to bed on Sept. 11.

What started out as a steady rain suddenly turned savage shortly before midnight. Rain showers intensified and kept coming in ever-stronger torrents.

Within a matter of hours, many residents along Fish Creek Road were desperately trying to save their homes and their lives.

Evacuations of threatened residents began during the early hours of Sept. 12 throughout the east side of Estes Park and in parts of the Big Thompson Canyon.

Fall River rose quickly and began to leave its banks around 6:30 a.m. Within an hour, there was approximately 2 feet of water racing down Elkhorn Avenue and splashing up against storefront doors.

Over the next 24 hours, 4½ miles of Fish Creek Road would be washed away into Lake Estes. Along with it would go water, sewer, and other utilities, impacting about 2,000 people.

It would be the worst natural disaster the town has faced since the 1982 Lawn Lake flood or the 1976 Big Thompson Canyon flood.

---

**LEFT:** Fish Creek rushes past Scott Avenue, taking part of the street downstream on Thursday, Sept. 12. The East side of Fish Creek was isolated by the flood, as the normally small creek washed away streets and bridges. WALT HESTER/ESTES PARK TRAIL-GAZETTE

**RIGHT:** Volunteers help one another across fast-moving water on Elkhorn Avenue on Thursday evening, Sept. 12. Residents got together to help sandbag businesses downtown and keep one another as safe as possible. WALT HESTER/ESTES PARK TRAIL-GAZETTE

**BOTTOM LEFT:** Volunteers slog through dirty water to place sandbags along East Elkhorn Avenue on Thursday night, Sept. 12. WALT HESTER/ESTES PARK TRAIL-GAZETTE

**BOTTOM RIGHT:** A house with people still inside is surrounded by Fish Creek on Thursday, Sept. 12. Flooding closed roads and neighborhoods around Estes Park as heavy rain soaked the entire Front Range. WALT HESTER/ESTES PARK TRAIL-GAZETTE

**OPPOSITE:** A normally tiny stream floods the police station parking lot on Saturday, Sept. 12. WALT HESTER/ESTES PARK TRAIL-GAZETTE

Estes Park's number 1 news and advertising source | 75 cents | Wednesday, September 18, 2013 | eptrail.com

## Estes Park opening up after flood

Page 5

## Local sports scene put on hold

Page 7

# ESTES PARK
# Trail Gazette

» EPTRAIL.COM: NEWS, VIDEO AND PHOTOS OF THE ESTES VALLEY

# Estes Park begins recovery effort

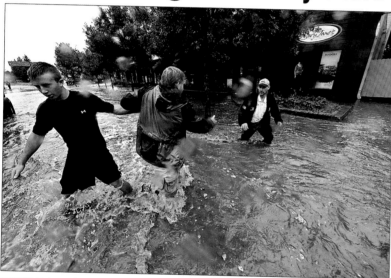

Volunteers help each other across fast-moving water on Elkhorn Ave. on Thursday evening. Residents got together to help sandbag businesses downtown and keep each other as safe as possible.
*Walt Hester / Trail-Gazette*

## Citizens, town turn to massive task of rebuilding

By David Persons
Trail-Gazette

Even as Estes Park residents and business owners struggle with issues like water, sewage, washed-out roads, barricades, and more, the town's recovery effort from last week's devastating, multi-day, flash flood event is well underway.

The problem, however, is that very little will be a quick fix. Some things will take months to fix. Others will take longer.

"It will take years of construction to put everything
See **RECOVERY**, pg. 3

Friends and volunteers begin removing mud from Outdoor World on Saturday. Clean up began almost as soon as rain stopped falling, as Estes Park residents and businesses remover mud and debris.
*Walt Hester / Trail-Gazette*

## Sept. storm resulted in historic flooding, damage

### Cost to areas devastated by flooding expected to be in billions

By David Persons
Trail-Gazette

The cost of last week's catastrophic flash flooding that devastated parts of Estes Park, Glen Haven, the Big Thompson Canyon, Lyons, Boulder and scores of other Front Range mountain communities, will likely run into the

billions of dollars, say state officials.

The time it will take to fix some roads and bridges could take months, a year, maybe even longer, state highway officials are saying.

Assessments of the damage to Estes Park homes, businesses and infrastructure is still ongoing. No damage cost estimates are available yet.

For a short time late last week, Estes Park was cut off from the rest of the state as all its main roads were seriously damaged
See **STORM**, pg. 2

## Wedding rainout

By David Persons
Trail-Gazette

Nicole Ranalletta has a love affair with Estes Park, its mountains, its trees, its streams, its dramatic beau-

That marriage would have taken place this Sunday at the Estes Park Resort.

But, last week's historic flooding event washed out all those plans.

As a result, it wasn't an

## Town may be isolated for long time

By Bianca Prieto
Digital First Media -
Trail-Gazette

Estes Park could remain isolated for months as officials work to re-open major

**LEFT:** Staff members of the Wind River Ranch await places to stay after evacuation from the ranch. The staff was placed with families in Estes Park.
WALT HESTER/ESTES PARK TRAIL-GAZETTE

**OPPOSITE RIGHT:** Two women test to see how close they can get to their shops on Friday. Rising water from the Fall River divided parts of town, making travel dangerous or even impossible on Friday, Sept. 13.
WALT HESTER/ESTES PARK TRAIL-GAZETTE

**BOTTOM LEFT:** Curious residents check out rain and mud at Elkhorn and Moraine avenues.
WALT HESTER/ESTES PARK TRAIL-GAZETTE

**BOTTOM RIGHT:** A woman has a hard time looking at the destruction on Elkhorn Avenue on Friday, Sept. 13. Most of the businesses in the downtown section of Elkhorn Avenue suffered damage from the historic flood.
WALT HESTER/ESTES PARK TRAIL-GAZETTE

**ABOVE:** An Estes Park Public Works official documents the breach in the lower Scott Pond on Friday morning, Sept. 13. The dam failure added more water to the already overflowing Fish Creek. WALT HESTER/ESTES PARK TRAIL-GAZETTE

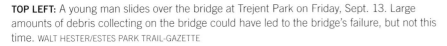

**TOP LEFT:** A young man slides over the bridge at Trejent Park on Friday, Sept. 13. Large amounts of debris collecting on the bridge could have led to the bridge's failure, but not this time. WALT HESTER/ESTES PARK TRAIL-GAZETTE

**ABOVE:** Fish Creek was a raging torrent flowing down Fish Creek Road on Saturday morning, Sept. 14. The creek had breached its banks in nine locations. JOHN CORDSEN/ESTES PARK TRAIL-GAZETTE

**TOP RIGHT AND RIGHT:** Friends and volunteers begin removing mud from Outdoor World on Saturday, Sept. 14. Cleanup began almost as soon as rain stopped falling, as Estes Park residents and businesses removed mud and debris. WALT HESTER/ESTES PARK TRAIL-GAZETTE

**RIGHT:** A sinkhole compromises the road into the YMCA of the Rockies after the historic rain and flash flooding. The rains undercut several sections of Spur 66 and breached the dam that held back Dorsey Lake.
WALT HESTER/ESTES PARK TRAIL-GAZETTE

**BOTTOM LEFT:** A bridge over the Big Thompson River sits damaged and unusable on Saturday, Sept. 14, isolating the Glacier Lodge. The bridge withstood years of spring runoff only to be nearly swept away by floodwaters this week. WALT HESTER/ESTES PARK TRAIL-GAZETTE

**BOTTOM MIDDLE:** A trout floats in a bottle at the YMCA of the Rockies on Saturday, Sept. 14. Fish were stranded on streets in the area after the floodwaters receded.
WALT HESTER/ESTES PARK TRAIL-GAZETTE

**BOTTOM RIGHT:** A worker uses a chain saw to break up a tree lodged under a footbridge over the Big Thompson River on Monday morning, Sept. 16, in Estes Park.
JOHN CORDSEN/ESTES PARK TRAIL-GAZETTE

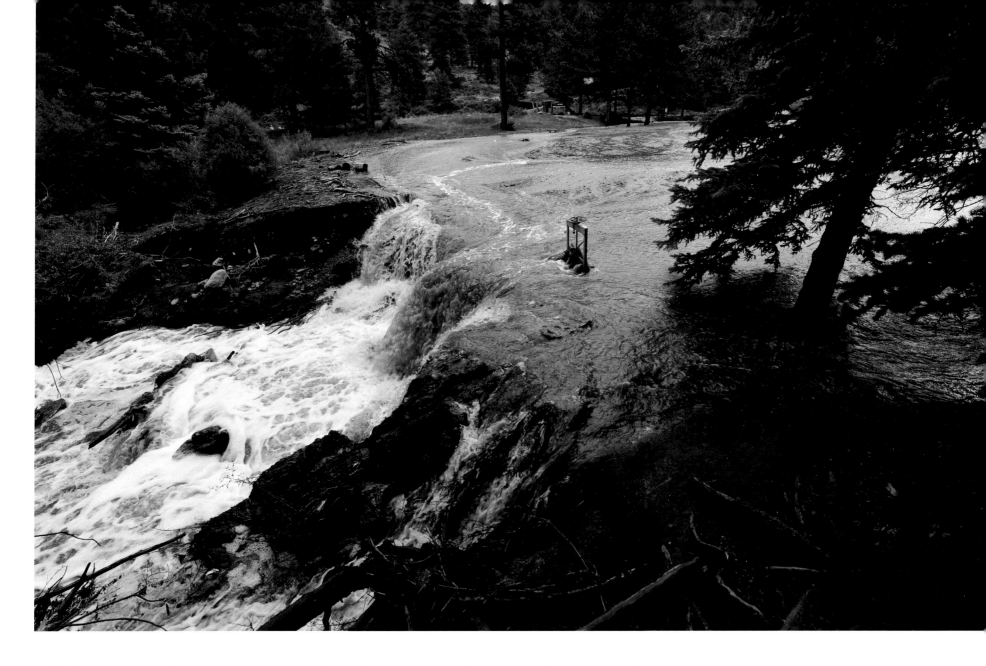

**ABOVE:** Water streams out of Dorsey Lake on Saturday, Sept. 14, after the dam was breached by floodwaters. While the road and the small pond were damaged, only minor water damage was reported at the YMCA of the Rockies. WALT HESTER/ESTES PARK TRAIL-GAZETTE

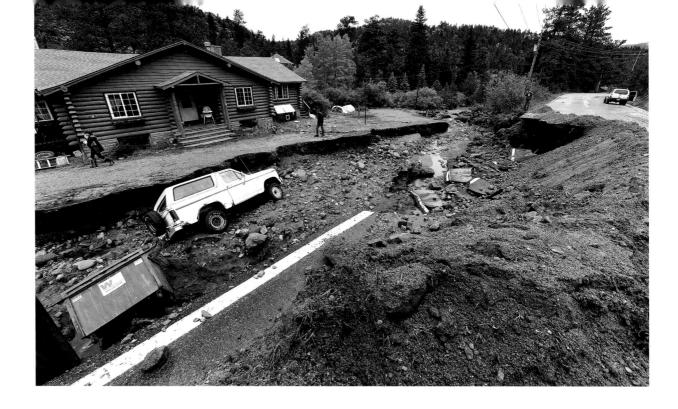

**RIGHT:** A trash bin and an SUV rest in a gully above Glen Haven. Roads, property and lives were lost in the flood. WALT HESTER/ESTES PARK TRAIL-GAZETTE

**BOTTOM LEFT:** Workers unload a National Guard Chinook helicopter at the Stanley Fairgrounds on Friday, Sept. 13. The huge helicopters were used to evacuate people and move supplies around the Front Range during the flood and early recovery efforts. WALT HESTER/ESTES PARK TRAIL-GAZETTE

**BOTTOM RIGHT:** An Estes Park Light and Power worker flings a cable to a co-worker in Glen Haven on Wednesday, Sept. 18. Most of the community's infrastructure, as well as buildings, were destroyed in the flood. WALT HESTER/ESTES PARK TRAIL-GAZETTE

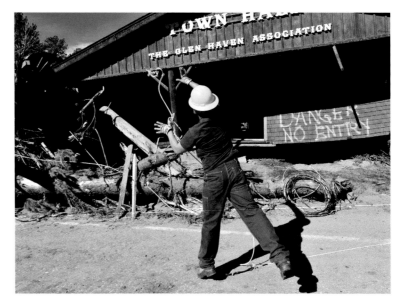

Estes Park's number 1 news and advertising source | 75 cents | Friday, September 20, 2013 | eptrail.com

## Neighbors helping neighbors

Page 6

## Around the 'Horn' in the national park

Page 9

# ESTES PARK
# Trail Gazette

» EPTRAIL.COM: NEWS, VIDEO AND PHOTOS OF THE ESTES VALLEY

# Businesses spring back to life after flood

### Hard-hit sections of Elkhorn digging out, looking to reopen

By David Persons
Trail-Gazette

Estes Park was a beehive of activity on Wednesday and Thursday as downtown merchants and business owners throughout the flood-impacted areas scrambled to get up and running again.

That was no more apparent than on Elkhorn Ave.

Scores of merchants were pulling out carpet, scrubbing floors, emptying flooded basements and washing down sidewalks.

A handful of businesses were even open for business.

One of those was Moosely T's and Sports, 124 E. Elkhorn.

Owner Jerri Paulson stood in the doorway, greeting friends, and smiling as people began strolling down the sidewalk.

"We didn't have any real damage," Paulson said.

"Some mud and a little water came under the front door but it just collected on the carpet mat. I just rolled it up and took it out. That's it."

Paulson credited the new doors that the building's owner put on the business four months ago for being able to keep the 3-foot deluge of water that raced down Elkhorn from entering her business.

Amy Hamrick, the owner of Kind Coffee, 470 E. Elkhorn, had the opposite luck.

Kind Coffee sits at the bottom of E. Elkhorn along side Fall River. All the water that came down Elkhorn Ave., raced into her parking lot and across her property before joining up with Fall River just outside the east wall of her business.

The geographic location of her business gave her a frightening, front row seat of the flood.

"Last Thursday, I got here at 5:45 a.m. and was going to open at 6:30," Hamrick said. "The river was running high but it wasn't flooding. But, it did look scary, like a high spring runoff."

Hamrick eventually left about 2 p.m.

Despite the damage, Hamrick plans to reopen as soon as she can. In the meantime, she wants to thank all those who helped her save her business.

"I got so much help from the community, customers, people I've never met," she said.

"About 8 or 8:30, the parking lot (which faces Elkhorn) filled up very fast," Hamrick said.

Then the river came out of its banks and water rose quickly around her business. She said some customers left, others stayed to help her get inventory off the floor.

Despite getting about 12-15 inches of water in her building, she was able to "prevent as much loss as possible" by moving computers, plugging and unplugging things.

Up and down Elkhorn, it was the same story – one business had little damage, while another had serious damage.

Trendz at the Park, 100 E. Elkhorn (on the southeast corner of Elkhorn and Moraine), should have been buried in water and muck. It

Friends of Kind Coffee help dry carpets in the coffee shop. As the sunshine returns, resolute Estes Park residents are hard at work to bring business back.
*Walt Hester / Trail-Gazette*

Sixteen inches of water fills the basement of the Hiking Hut on Saturday. The business, which was one of the first to reopen after the Mail Fire, found much of their back stock ruined by the flood.
*Walt Hester / Trail-Gazette*

See BUSINESSES, pg. 2

# Feds free up another $30M for area road, bridge repair

Fish Creek rushes past Scott Avenue, taking part of the street down stream last Thursday. The floodwaters left extensive road damage in their wake, prompting the feds to allocated funds for repairs.

By David Persons
Trail-Gazette

U.S. Transportation Secretary Anthony Foxx today announced that the U.S. Department of Transportation is immediately making available an additional $30 million in emergency relief funds to help Colorado cover the costs of repairing roads

to Colorado follows 85 million from the department last week, bringing the total to $35 million.

Sen. Michael Bennet's office made the announcement to Estes Park officials

early today and told them the top priorities for spending the money will be to fix U.S. Highways 34, 36, Colo. Highways 7, 14 and Larimer County Road 43.

"Thank you, Sen. Bennet,"

See REPAIR, pg. 2

Volume 44, NO. 25

### Index
Local .................... 1
Opinion ............... 4

---

Estes Park's number 1 news and advertising source | 75 cents | Friday, September 27, 2013 | eptrail.com

## Stanley plan deserves a chance

Page 4

## Let the games begin - again

Page 11

# ESTES PARK
# Trail Gaze

» EPTRAIL.COM: NEWS, VIDEO AND PHOTOS OF THE ESTES VALLEY

# Flood bill for Estes Park could be $40M

### Tab is for public infrastructure, not private residences

By David Persons
Trail-Gazette

Estes Park Town Administrator Frank Lancaster revealed Wednesday that the preliminary cost of replacing damaged infrastructure in the town could be as high as $40 million.

Lancaster, addressing the public in the final scheduled town hall briefing, said the damage estimate was reached after meeting with Federal Emergency Management Administration (FEMA) officials.

"That's just public infrastructure, not private residences," Lancaster said.

Lancaster said that all the damage was being carefully documented in order for the town to receive funding from outside agencies.

The town administrator also pointed out that FEMA will not be able to fund all of the town's losses.

"FEMA will fund 75 percent but the other 25 percent will have to come from matches," he said. "So, of the $40 million, the town will have to come up with 25 per-

cent ($10 million). We just don't have that in our coffers. We're hoping the state

will be able to help with some of that and maybe we can get some in-kind matches.

"We're trying to work on that and be as creative as we

can."

Lancaster said while the recovery is moving forward

as fast as possible, the Fish

A convoy of heavy road-building equipment makes its way from the west side of Rocky Mountain National Park into Estes Park through Horseshoe Park on Wednesday. The equipment will be used to rebuild Fish Creek Road among others.
*Walt Hester / Trail-Gazette*

See FLOOD, pg. 3

# Top candidate for CEO emerges

### Oregon man identified as top CEO candidate for Estes Park Medical Center

By David Persons
Trail-Gazette

Brian Herwig, a chief operating officer with a Medford, Ore. hospital, has emerged as the top candidate to fill the role of Chief Executive Officer at Estes Park Medical Center.

board meeting has been scheduled for 3 p.m. Oct. 1 to vote on hiring Herwig.

Van Der Ploeg, who headed up the search team, said that Herwig's name kept coming up as the team sifted through the nearly 200 candidates.

"It was a lot of work but a very pleasant experience," Van Der Ploeg said of the search that started shortly after former CEO Robb Austin resigned in January. Bobbi Swenson has been the medical center's interim

Estes Park Medical Center

# Stanley owner proposes bold development

### Proposal calls for $15 million wellness center to be built near the hotel

By David Persons
Trail-Gazette

Stanley Hotel owner John Cullen announced late Tuesday his plans for a $15 million wellness center facility to be built on land near the hotel.

Cullen said he is partnering with the Anschutz Medical Center in Aurora to create the Stanley Hotel/Anschutz Medical Center for Wellness. A similar facility is also being

The Stanley Master Plan

CAMPUS ZONES
- HOTEL ZONE
- SUSTAINABILITY ZONE
- WELLNESS ZONE

*Courtesy Photo*

# Acknowledgments

**Al Manzi**
President, publisher and CEO, Prairie Mountain Media

**Jill Stravolemos**
VP Marketing & Advertising, Prairie Mountain Media

**Dan Anderson**
VP Finance, Prairie Mountain Media

**Kevin Kaufman**
Executive editor, Daily Camera;
VP News, Prairie Mountain Media

**Dean Lehman**
Publisher, Longmont Times-Call,
Loveland Reporter-Herald

**Mike Romero**
Publisher, Estes Park Trail-Gazette

**Paul Aiken**
Photo editor, Prairie Mountain Media

**Matt Sebastian**
City editor, Daily Camera

**John Vahlenkamp**
Managing editor, Longmont Times-Call

**Jeff Stahla**
Managing editor, Loveland Reporter-Herald

**John Cordsen**
Editor, Estes Park Trail-Gazette

## Special thanks to:

**We especially want to recognize the** amazing staffs of all our Prairie Mountain Media publications across Colorado, particularly those in the paths of the flooding, who — while many themselves faced personal flooding threats — covered the news 24/7 for our readers, assisted our many clients in their time of need and kept our operations running. We could not be prouder of every member of our team.

Additionally, we want to recognize the amazing efforts of our local law enforcement and emergency response/rescue teams, the host of relief workers and rescue crews on scene to help with this disaster, our friends and neighbors throughout our communities and the countless nonprofits and volunteers who self-lessly lent a hand to any in need.

## Purchase photos:

To purchase individual photos from this book, visit http://bit.ly/coflood or scan this QR code with your smartphone:

# Our photojournalists

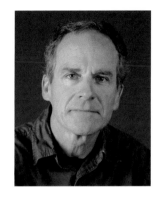

**Paul Aiken**
Photo editor, Prairie Mountain
Media and Daily Camera

**Matt Jonas**
Photo editor,
Longmont Times-Call

**Jenny Sparks**
Photo editor,
Loveland Reporter-Herald

**Lewis Geyer**
Photojournalist,
Longmont Times-Call

**Cliff Grassmick**
Photojournalist,
Daily Camera

**Walt Hester**
Photojournalist,
Estes Park Trail-Gazette

**Dave Jennings**
Photojournalist,
Broomfield Enterprise

**Mark Leffingwell**
Photojournalist,
Daily Camera

**Greg Lindstrom**
Photojournalist,
Longmont Times-Call

**Lilia Muñoz**
Photojournalist intern,
Loveland Reporter-Herald

**Jeremy Papasso**
Photojournalist,
Daily Camera

**Steve Stoner**
Photojournalist, Loveland
Reporter-Herald

**Craig Young**
Reporter, Loveland
Reporter-Herald

# In Remembrance

We remember and honor our loved ones, friends and neighbors killed in the Colorado flood of 2013. You will be missed.

## Wiyanna Nelson, 19

...escribed by family and friends as creative, ...dhearted — graduated from Centaurus High ...2. She was with a group of friends returning ...friend's birthday party late the night of Sept. ... car became stuck in a mudslide on Linden ...of Boulder. Wiyanna, along with her boyfriend, ...nlan, was swept away by the floodwaters.

## Wesley Quinlan, 19

Wesley graduated from Centaurus High School in the spring. His family and friends described him as creative, passionate, kindhearted. He was with a group of friends returning from another friend's birthday party late the night of Sept. 11 when their car became stuck in a mudslide on Linden Drive just west of Boulder. Wesley, along with his girlfriend, Wiyanna Nelson, was swept away by the floodwaters.

## Joseph Howlett, 72

Joseph was the beloved former owner of Jamestown Mercantile. He was described by one friend as the guy "everybody" knew and a man who "wasn't afraid to share himself with people." He was killed on Sept. 12 when his home collapsed on him after it was pummeled by rushing waters.

## Gerald Boland, 80

...retired math teacher and highly respected ...e Lyons basketball coach. He was among the ...t Lyons Elementary and prepare it to serve as ...enter. Gerald's body was found a few hundred ...he family's Lyons home. He was killed while ...rching for his wife, Cheron, to ensure she was ...

## Evelyn Starner, 79

Evelyn worked in the rehabilitation department at the Good Samaritan Village in Loveland and commuted every day from her home in Cedar Cove. Described as the "den mother" of the staff at the retirement community, she had been named the Good Samaritan Society's CNA of the year in 2000. She is survived by three children, 10 grandchildren and five great-grandchildren. ...floodwaters destroyed her home.

## Patty Goodwine, 60

Patty worked at the Loveland Public Library for 34 years, where she was an executive administrative assistant. Those who worked with her described her as "the heart" of the library, bringing joy to those around her. She was swept away on Sept. 13 as the Big Thompson River destroyed her Cedar Cover home In the Big Thompson Canyon.